CAMBRIDGE LIBRARY COLLECTION

Books of enduring scholarly value

History of Medicine

It is sobering to realise that as recently as the year in which On the Origin of Species was published, learned opinion was that diseases such as typhus and cholera were spread by a 'miasma', and suggestions that doctors should wash their hands before examining patients were greeted with mockery by the profession. The Cambridge Library Collection reissues milestone publications in the history of Western medicine as well as studies of other medical traditions. Its coverage ranges from Galen on anatomical procedures to Florence Nightingale's common-sense advice to nurses, and includes early research into genetics and mental health, colonial reports on tropical diseases, documents on public health and military medicine, and publications on spa culture and medicinal plants.

Body and Mind

Yorkshireman Henry Maudsley (1835–1918) studied and built his medical career in London. From 1860 he specialised in psychiatry, working at hospitals and in private practice, and from 1863 to 1878 he was joint editor of the Journal of Mental Science. As one of the leading European 'alienists', he treated high-profile patients and became sufficiently wealthy to contribute £30,000 in 1907 towards the foundation of a specialist psychiatric hospital. In his many publications, he developed ideas of heredity derived from Darwin. His lecturing style was famous; Body and Mind contains his 1870 Gulstonian lectures, given before the Royal College of Physicians, and two earlier articles. Maudsley aimed to 'bring man, both in his physical and mental relations, as much as possible within the scope of scientific enquiry', and his preface dismisses 'vague and barren disputations concerning materialism and spiritualism' as futile compared to serious scientific enquiry based on physiology.

T0371299

Cambridge University Press has long been a pioneer in the reissuing of out-of-print titles from its own backlist, producing digital reprints of books that are still sought after by scholars and students but could not be reprinted economically using traditional technology. The Cambridge Library Collection extends this activity to a wider range of books which are still of importance to researchers and professionals, either for the source material they contain, or as landmarks in the history of their academic discipline.

Drawing from the world-renowned collections in the Cambridge University Library and other partner libraries, and guided by the advice of experts in each subject area, Cambridge University Press is using state-of-the-art scanning machines in its own Printing House to capture the content of each book selected for inclusion. The files are processed to give a consistently clear, crisp image, and the books finished to the high quality standard for which the Press is recognised around the world. The latest print-on-demand technology ensures that the books will remain available indefinitely, and that orders for single or multiple copies can quickly be supplied.

The Cambridge Library Collection brings back to life books of enduring scholarly value (including out-of-copyright works originally issued by other publishers) across a wide range of disciplines in the humanities and social sciences and in science and technology.

Body and Mind

*An Inquiry into their Connection and Mutual
Influence, Specially in Reference to Mental Disorders*

HENRY MAUDSLEY

CAMBRIDGE
UNIVERSITY PRESS

University Printing House, Cambridge, CB2 8BS, United Kingdom

Cambridge University Press is part of the University of Cambridge.
It furthers the University's mission by disseminating knowledge in the pursuit of
education, learning and research at the highest international levels of excellence.

www.cambridge.org
Information on this title: www.cambridge.org/9781108080309

This edition first published 1870
This digitally printed version 2017

ISBN 978-1-108-08030-9 Paperback

BODY AND MIND.

BODY AND MIND:

AN INQUIRY INTO THEIR CONNECTION AND MUTUAL INFLUENCE, SPECIALLY IN REFERENCE TO MENTAL DISORDERS;

BEING THE

GULSTONIAN LECTURES FOR 1870,

DELIVERED BEFORE THE ROYAL COLLEGE OF PHYSICIANS.

WITH APPENDIX.

BY

HENRY MAUDSLEY, M.D. LOND.

FELLOW OF THE ROYAL COLLEGE OF PHYSICIANS ;
PROFESSOR OF MEDICAL JURISPRUDENCE IN UNIVERSITY COLLEGE, LONDON ;
PRESIDENT-ELECT OF THE MEDICO-PSYCHOLOGICAL ASSOCIATION ;
HONORARY MEMBER OF THE MEDICO-PSYCHOLOGICAL SOCIETY OF PARIS,
OF THE IMPERIAL SOCIETY OF PHYSICIANS OF VIENNA, AND OF THE SOCIETY FOR THE
PROMOTION OF PSYCHIATRY AND FORENSIC PSYCHOLOGY OF VIENNA.
FORMERLY RESIDENT PHYSICIAN OF THE MANCHESTER ROYAL LUNATIC HOSPITAL, ETC.

London:

MACMILLAN AND CO.

1870.

LONDON :
R. CLAY, SONS, AND TAYLOR, PRINTERS,
BREAD STREET HILL.

PREFACE.

THE three lectures forming the first part of this volume
were delivered before the Royal College of Physicians of
London, to which I had the honour of being appointed
Gulstonian Lecturer for this year ; the latter part consists
of two articles which, having appeared elsewhere, are
reprinted here as presenting a completer view of some
points that are only touched upon in the lectures ; and
the general plan of the whole, as thus constituted, may be
described as being to bring man, both in his physical and
mental relations, as much as possible within the scope of
scientific inquiry.

The first lecture is devoted to a general survey of the
Physiology of Mind—to an exposition of the physical
conditions of mental function in health.   In the second
lecture are sketched the features of some forms of

degeneracy of mind, as exhibited in morbid varieties of the human kind, with the purpose of bringing prominently into notice the operation of physical causes from generation to generation, and the relationship of mental to other disorders of the nervous system. In the third lecture, which contains a general survey of the pathology of mind, are displayed the relations of morbid states of the body to disordered mental function. I would fain believe the general result to be a well-warranted conclusion that, whatever theories may be held concerning mind and the best method of its study, it is vain to expect, and a folly to attempt, to rear a stable fabric of mental science, without taking faithful account of physiological and pathological inquiries into its phenomena.

In the criticism of the "Limits of Philosophical Inquiry," which follows the lectures, will be found reasons why no attempt has been made to discuss the bearing of the views. broached in them on any system of philosophy. Neither materialism nor spiritualism are scientific terms, and one need have no concern with them in a scientific inquiry, which, if it be true to its spirit, is bound to have regard only to what lies within its powers and to the truth of its results. It would seem to be full time that vague and barren disputations concerning materialism and spiritualism should end, and that, instead of continuing such fruitless and unprofitable discussion, men should apply themselves diligently to discover, by direct inter-rogation of nature, how much matter can do without spiritual help. Let each investigator pursue the method of research which most suits the bent of his genius, and here, as in other departments of science, let each system be judged by its fruits, which cannot fail in the end to be the best sponsors and sureties for its truth. But the physiological inquirer into mind may, if he care to do so, justly protest against the easy confidence with which some metaphysical psychologists disdain physiological inquiry, and ignore its results, without ever having been at the pains to make themselves acquainted with what these results are, and with the steps by which they have been reached. Let theory be what it may, there can be no just question of the duty of observing faithfully all the instances which mental phenomena offer for inductive inquiry, and of striving to realize the entirely new aspect which an exact study of the physiology of the nervous system gives to many problems of mental science. One reflection cannot fail to occur forcibly to those who have pursued this study, namely, that it would have been well could the physiological inquirer, after rising step by step from the investigation of life in its lowest forms to that of its highest and most complex manifestations, have entered upon his investigations of mind without being hampered by any philosophical theories concerning it. The very terms of metaphysical psychology have, instead of helping, oppressed and hindered him to an extent which it is impossible to measure : they have been hobgoblins to frighten him from entering on his path of inquiry, phantoms to lead him astray at every turn after he has entered upon it, deceivers lurking to betray him under the guise of seeming friends tendering help. Let him take all the pains in the world, he cannot express adequately and exactly what he would—neither more nor less—for he must use words which have already meanings of a metaphysical kind attached to them, and which, when used, are therefore for him more or less a misinterpretation. He is thus forced into an apparent encroachment on questions which he does not in the least degree wish to meddle with, and provokes an antagonism without ever designing it ; and so one cannot but think it would have been well if he could have had his own words exactly fitting his facts, and free from the vagueness and ambiguity of a former metaphysical use.

The article on the " Theory of Vitality," which appeared in 1863, is now reprinted, with a few, mainly verbal, alterations. The aspect of some of the questions discussed in it has been somewhat changed by the progress of inquiry and thought since that time, but it appears to the Author that, great as discussion has been, there are yet considerations respecting vitality that have not been duly weighed. Whether living matter was formed originally, or is now being formed, from non-living matter, by the operation of physical causes and natural laws, are questions which, notwithstanding the lively and vigorous handling which they have had, are far from being settled. Exact experiment can alone put an end to this dispute : the one conclusive experiment, indeed, in proof of the origin of living from dead matter, will be to make life. Meanwhile, as the subject is still in the region of discussion, it is permissible to set forth the reflections which the facts seem to warrant, and to endeavour to indicate the direction of scientific develop-ment which seems to be foretokened by, or to exist potentially in, the knowledge which we have thus far acquired. This much may be said : that those who oppose the doctrine of so-called spontaneous generation, not on the ground of the absence of conclusive evidence of its occurrence, which they might justly do, but on the ground of what they consider special characteristics of living matter, would do well to look with more insight into the phenomena of non-living nature, and to consider more deeply what they see, in order to discover whether the characteristic properties of life are quite so special and exclusive as they imagine them to be. Having done that, they might go on to consider whether, even if their premises were granted, any conclusion regarding the mode of origin of life would legitimately follow; whether in fact it would not be entirely gratuitous and unwarrantable to conclude thence the impossibility of the origin of living matter from non-living matter. The etymological import of the words physics and physiology is notably the same; and it may be that, as has been suggested, in the difference of their application lies a hidden irony at the assumption on which the division is grounded.

> 9, HANOVER SQUARE, W.
> *November* 5, 1870.

CONTENTS.

LECTURES.

PAGE

1. ON THE PHYSICAL CONDITION OF MENTAL FUNCTION
   IN HEALTH I

2. ON CERTAIN FORMS OF DEGENERACY OF MIND, THEIR
   CAUSATION, AND THEIR RELATIONS TO OTHER
   DISORDERS OF THE NERVOUS SYSTEM 40

3. ON THE RELATIONS OF MORBID BODILY STATES TO
   DISORDERED MENTAL FUNCTIONS 77

APPENDIX.

1. THE LIMITS OF PHILOSOPHICAL INQUIRY 115
2. THE THEORY OF VITALITY 143

LECTURES.

1. ON THE PHYSICAL CONDITION OF MENTAL FUNCTION IN HEALTH.

2. ON CERTAIN FORMS OF DEGENERACY OF MIND, THEIR CAUSATION, AND THEIR RELATIONS TO OTHER DISORDERS OF THE NERVOUS SYSTEM.

3. ON THE RELATIONS OF MORBID BODILY STATES TO DISORDERED MENTAL FUNCTIONS.

BODY AND MIND:

AN INQUIRY INTO THEIR CONNECTION AND MUTUAL INFLUENCE, SPECIALLY IN REFERENCE TO MENTAL DISORDERS.

LECTURE I.

GENTLEMEN,—The relations of mind and body in health and in disease I have chosen as the subject of these Lectures, not with the hope of doing full justice to so complex and difficult an inquiry, but because it has for some time been my special work, and there was no other subject on which I should have felt myself equally justified in addressing you. No one can be more deeply sensible than I am how little exact our knowledge is of the bodily conditions of mental functions, and how much of that which we think we know is vague, uncertain, and fluctuating. But the time has come when the immediate business which lies before anyone who would advance our knowledge of mind unquestionably is a close and searching scrutiny of the bodily conditions of its manifestations in health and disease. It is most necessary now to make use of the results of the study of mind in health to light and guide our researches into its morbid phenomena, and in like manner to bring the instructive instances presented by unsound mind to bear upon the interpretation of its healthy functions. The physiology and the pathology of mind are two branches of one science; and he who studies the one must, if he would work wisely and well, study the other also. My aim will be to promote the reconciliation between them, and in doing so I shall embrace the occasion, whenever it offers itself, to indicate the principles which should guide our efforts for what must always be the highest object of medical science and art,—the production and preservation of a sound mind in a sound body. Actually to accomplish much of this purpose will not lie in my power, but I may bring together fragmentary observations, point out the bearing of them on one another and on received opinions, thus unfold their meaning, and mark broadly the lines which future research must take.

Within the memory of men now living insanity was such a special study, and its treatment such a special art, that it stood quite aloof from general medicine in a mysterious and mischievous isolation; owing little or nothing to the results of progress in other branches of medicine, and contributing nothing to their progress. The reason of this it is not hard to discover. The habit of viewing mind as an intangible entity or incorporeal essence, which science inherited from theology, prevented men from subjecting its phenomena to the same method of investigation as other natural phenomena ; its disorders were thought to be an incomprehensible affliction and, in accordance with the theological notion, due to the presence of an evil spirit in the sufferer, or to the enslavement of the soul by sin, or to anything but their true cause—bodily disease. Consequently, the treatment of the insane was not in the hands of intelligent physicians, who aimed to apply the resources of medicine to the alleviation or cure of bodily illness, but was given up to coarse and ignorant gaolers, whose savage cruelties will for all time to come be a great and ugly blot upon the enlightenment of the age which tolerated them.

Matters are happily changed now.   On all hands it is admitted that the manifestations of mind take place through the nervous system ; and that its derangements are the result of nervous disease, amenable to the same method of investigation as other nervous diseases.   Insanity has accordingly become a strictly medical study, and its treatment a branch of medical practice.   Still, it is all too true that, notwithstanding we know much, and are day by day learning more, of the physiology of the nervous system, we are only on the threshold of the study of it as an instrument subserving mental function.   We know little more positively than that it has such function ; we know nothing whatever of the physics and of the chemistry of thought.   The conception of mind as a mysterious entity, different essentially from, and vastly superior to, the body which it inhabits and uses as its earthly tenement, but from which its noblest aspirations are thought to be to get free, still works openly or in a latent way to obstruct the study of its functions by the methods of physical research. Without speculating at all concerning the nature of mind,—which, let me distinctly declare at the outset, is a question which science cannot touch, and I do not dream of attempting to touch, —I do not shrink from saying that we shall make no progress towards a mental science if we begin by depreciating the body : not by disdaining it, as metaphysicians, religious ascetics, and maniacs have done, but by labouring in an earnest and inquiring spirit to understand it, shall we make any step forward ; and when we have fully comprehended its functions, when we know how to estimate fitly this highest, most complex, and wonderful achievement of organized skill, it will be quite time, if there be then the inclination, to look down upon it with contempt.

The truth is that in inquiries concerning mind, as was once the case in speculations concerning other natural phenomena or forces, it has been the practice to begin where the inquiry should have ended. Just as the laws of physical actions were evoked out of the depths of human consciousness, and the relations of bodies to one another attributed to sympathies and antipathies, attractions and abhorrences, instead of being acquired by patient observation and careful generalization, so has a fabric of mental philosophy been reared on the doubtful revelations of self-consciousness, in entire disregard of the more tedious and less attractive duty of observation of facts, and induction from them. Surely it is time we put seriously to ourselves the question whether the inductive method, which has proved its worth by its abundant fruitfulness wherever it has been faithfully applied, should not be as rigidly used in the investigation of mind as in the investigation of other natural phenomena. If so, we ought certainly to begin our inquiry with the observation of the simplest instances—with its physiological manifestations in animals, in children, in idiots, in savages, mounting by degrees to the highest and most recondite facts of consciousness, the interpretation or the misinterpretation of which constitutes what has hitherto claimed to be mental philosophy. The inductions which we get by observing the simple may be used with success to disentangle the phenomena of the complex ; but the endeavour to apply the complex and obscure to the interpretation of the simple is sure to end in confusion and error. The higher mental faculties are formed by evolution from the more simple and elementary, just as the more special and complex structure proceeds from the more simple and general ; and in the one case as in the other we must, if we would truly learn, follow the order of development. Not that it is within my present purpose to trace the plan of development of our mental faculties, but the facts and arguments which I shall bring forward will prove how vain and futile it is to strive to rear a sound fabric of mental science on any other foundation.

To begin the study of mind, then, with the observation of its humblest bodily manifestations, is a strictly scientific method. When we come to inquire what these are, it is far from easy to fix the point at which mental func-

tion begins. Without doubt most of the actions of man,
and many of those of the higher animals, do evince the
operation of mind, but whereabouts in the animal kingdom it first appears, and what part it has in the lower nerve
functions of man, are questions not easily answered. The
more closely the matter is looked into, the more clearly
it appears that we habitually embrace in our conception
of mind different nervous functions, some of which proceed from different nerve-centres, and the more necessary
it becomes to analyse these functions, to separate the more
simple and elementary, and to discover in the concrete
as much as possible of the meaning of the abstraction.
Is the brain the exclusive organ of mind? If it be so, to
what category of functions shall we refer the reflex acts
of the spinal cord, which take place independently of the
brain, and which often achieve as definite an end, and
seem to display as intelligent an aim, as any conscious
act of volition? It needs not to illustrate in detail the
nature and extent of reflex action, which is familiar
enough, but I may select a striking example in order to
serve as a text for the reflections which I wish to bring
forward. One simple fact, rightly understood and truly
interpreted, will teach as much as a thousand facts of the
same kind, but the thousand must have been previously
observed in order to understand truly the one ; for it is
certainly true that to apprehend the full meaning of
common things, it is necessary to study a great many
uncommon things. This, however, has been done in
this instance by the distinguished physiologists whose
labours have fixed on a tolerably firm basis the doctrine

of reflex action; we may, therefore, take as our starting-point the accepted results of their labours.

It is well known that if the hind foot of a frog that has had its head cut off be pinched, it is withdrawn from the irritation. The stimulus to the afferent nerve reaches the grey matter of the spinal cord, and sets free a force which excites to action the corresponding motor nerves of the same side. When the foot is pinched more strongly, the force liberated by the stimulus passes across the cord to the motor nerves of the opposite side, and there is a simultaneous withdrawal of both limbs; and if the excitation be stronger still, there is a wider irradiation of the effects of the stimulus in the grey matter, and a movement of all four limbs follows, the frog jumping away. These movements of the decapitated frog, which it is plain effect the definite purpose of getting it out of the way of harm, we believe to be analogous to the violent coughing by which food that has gone the wrong way is expelled from the human larynx, or to the vomiting by which offending matter is ejected from the stomach. Independently of consciousness and of will, an organism plainly has the power—call it intelligent or call it what we will—of feeling and eschewing what is hurtful to it, as well as of feeling and ensuing what is beneficial to it.

But the experiment on the frog may be made more striking and instructive. Touch with acetic acid the thigh of a decapitated frog over the internal condyle, and the animal rubs it off with the dorsal surface of the foot of the same side; cut off the foot, and apply the

acid to the same spot, and the animal tries to get at
it again with its foot, but of course, having lost it, cannot. After some fruitless efforts, therefore, it gives up
trying in that way, seems restless, as though, says
Pflüger, it was seeking some other way; and at last it
makes use of the foot of the other leg, and succeeds
in rubbing off the acid. Notably we have here not
merely contractions of muscles, but combined and har-
monized contractions in due sequence for a special
purpose. There are actions that have all the appearance
of being guided by intelligence and instigated by will
in an animal the recognized organ of whose intelligence
and will has been removed.

What are we to say in explanation of movements that
have such a look of adaptation? Are they mental, or
are they only physical? If they are mental, it is plain
that we must much enlarge and modify our conception
of mind, and of the seat of mind; if physical, it is plain
that we must subtract from mind functions that are
essential to its full function, and properties that are the
very foundations of its development in the higher centres. Some eminent physiologists now maintain, on the
strength of these experiments, that the accepted doctrine
of reflex action is quite untenable, and that the spinal cord
is really endowed with sensation and volition; and certainly these adapted actions seem to give us all the signs
of being felt and willed, except telling us that they are so.
Before accepting, however, this explanation of the obscure
by something more obscure still, it were well to realize
distinctly how dangerous a practice it usually is to apply

deductively to the interpretation of simple phenomena ideas pertaining to the more complex, and how essential a principle of the method of induction it is to follow the order of evolution, and to ascend from the interpretation of the simple to that of the complex. The explanation savours of the old and evil tendency which has done so much harm in philosophy, the tendency to explain the facts of nature by what we feel to go on in our minds; because we know that most of our actions take place consciously and voluntarily, we can hardly help thinking that it must be the same in the frog. Might we not, however, as well suppose and hold that positive attracts negative and repels positive electricity consciously and voluntarily, or that in the double decomposition of chemical salts one acid chooses voluntarily the other base? It is most necessary to be on our guard against the danger of misapplying ideas derived from internal observation of the functions of mind-centres to the interpretation of the functions of lower nerve-centres, and so of misinterpreting them. Assuredly we have sad experience enough to warn us against involving the latter in the metaphysical haze which still hangs over the functions of the supreme centres.

All the conclusion which the facts warrant is that actions for a definite end, having indeed the semblance of predesigning consciousness and will, may be quite unconscious and automatic; that the movements of the decapitated frog, adapted as they are to secure its wellbeing, are no more evidence of intelligence and will than are the movements of coughing, sneezing, and swallowing

in man.   In the constitution of the animal's spinal cord
are implanted the faculties of such movements for self-
preservation, which it has inherited as a part of its nature,
and without which it could hardly live a day ; accordingly
it acts necessarily and blindly; though it has lost its foot,
it endeavours vainly to act as if its foot was still there,
and only when the irritation continues unaffected by its
futile efforts makes, in answer to it, those further reflex
movements which are the physiological sequences of the
unsuccessful movements : it supplements one series of
reflex actions by another.[1]   But although these purposive
movements are not evidence of intelligence and volition
in the spinal cord, it is another question whether they
do not evince the same physiological properties and
the operation of the same laws of evolution as govern
the development of intelligence and will in the higher
centres.

   I have taken the experiment on the frog to exemplify
the proposition that designed actions may be unconscious
and automatic, because the phenomena are more simple
in it than in man, and more easy therefore to be understood ; but the proposition is equally true of his spinal
cord.   In its case, however, we have to bear in mind
that faculties are not innate to the same degree and
extent as in the lower animals, but have to be acquired
by education—to be organized, in fact, after birth.   It

[1] Wisely or unwisely, as the case may be ; for reflex movements
which commonly effect a useful end may, under the changed circumstances of disease, do great mischief, becoming even the occasion of
violent suffering and of a most painful death.

must be taught, just as the brain must, before it can perform its functions as an organ of animal life; and being much more under the control of the more highly developed brain, feeling and volition commonly mingle largely in its functions, and its independent action cannot be so plainly exhibited. But when its motor centres have been taught, when they have gained by education the power of executing what are called secondary automatic acts, it is certain that it can and does habitually execute them independently of consciousness and of will. They become as purely automatic as are the primitive reflex acts of the frog. To the statement, then, that actions bearing the semblance of design may be unconscious and automatic we have now to add a second and most weighty proposition—namely, that acts consciously designed at first may, by repetition, become unconscious and automatic, the faculties of them being organized in the constitution of the nerve-centres, and they being then performed as reflex effects of an external stimulus. This law, by which the education of the spinal cord takes place, is, as we shall hereafter see, a most important law in the development of the higher nerve-centres.

Let us now go a step further. The automatic acts, whether primary or secondary, in the frog or in the man, which are excited by the suitable external stimulus, may also be excited by an act of will, by an impulse coming downwards from the brain. When this happens, it should be clearly apprehended that the immediate agency of the movements is the same; it is in the motor centres of the spinal cord; the will does not and cannot act upon the nerve fibres of each muscle individually, but simply gives the order which sets in motion the organized machinery of the movements in the proper motor centres. This is a consideration of the utmost importance, for it exhibits how great a part of our voluntary acts is really the automatic action of the spinal cord. The same movements are effected by the same agency in answer to different stimuli—in the one case to an external stimulus, in the other case to an impulse of will; and in both cases the mind is alike ignorant of the immediate agency by which they are done. But while the automatic acts take place independently of will, the will is absolutely dependent on the organized experience in the cord for the accomplishment of its acts; without this it would be impotent to do a voluntary act. When therefore we have taken out of a voluntary act the large part which is due to the automatic agency of the motor centres, it clearly appears that we have subtracted no small proportion from what we are in the habit of comprising vaguely under mind. We perceive, indeed, how indispensable an exact and faithful observation of the functions of the spinal cord is to a true physiological inquiry into mind, and what an important means of analysis a knowledge of them yields us. Carrying the knowledge so gained into our examination of the functions of the higher nerve-centres, we observe how much of them it will serve to interpret. The result is that we find a great part of the habitual functions of the higher centres to be similarly automatic, and to admit of a similar physiological interpretation.

There can be no doubt that the ganglionic nuclei of the senses—the sensorial nuclei—are connected with motor nuclei; and that we have in such anatomical arrangement the agency of a number of reflex movements. Most of the instinctive acts of animals are of this kind, the faculties being innate in them. In man, however, who is actually the most helpless, though potentially the most powerful, of all living creatures when he comes into the world, the sensory and associated motor nuclei must be educated, just as the spinal centres must. To illustrate this sensori-motor or instinctive action, we may take the results of Flourens' well-known experiment of removing the cerebral hemispheres of a pigeon. What happens? The pigeon seemingly loses at once all intelligence and all power of spontaneous action. It appears as if it were asleep; yet, if thrown into the air, it will fly. If laid on its back, it struggles on to its legs again; the pupil of the eye contracts to light, and, if the light be very bright, the eyes are shut. It will dress its feathers if they are ruffled, and will sometimes follow with a movement of its head the movement of a candle before it; and, when a pistol is fired off, it will open its eyes, stretch its neck, raise its head, and then fall back into its former attitude. It is quite evident from this experiment that general sensibility and special sensations are possible after the removal of the hemispheres; but they are not then transformed into ideas. The impressions of sense reach and affect the sensory centres, but they are not intellectually *perceived;* and the proper movements are excited, but these are reflex or automatic. There are no ideas, there is no true spontaneity; and the animal would die of hunger before a plateful of food, though it will swallow it when pushed far enough into its mouth to come within the range of the reflex acts of deglutition. Here again, then, we have a surprising variety of adapted actions of which the body is capable without the intervention of intelligence, emotion, and will—without, in fact, mind in its exact sense having any part in them. The pigeon is brought to the level of the invertebrata, which have no higher nerve-centres than sensory ganglia, no centres of intelligence and will, and which execute all their varied and active movements, all their wonderful displays of instinct, through sensory and associated motor nuclei. They seek what is good for them, avoid what is hurtful to them, provide for the propagation of their kind—perform, indeed, all the functions of a very active life without *knowing* that they are doing so, not otherwise than as our pupils contract to light, or as our eyes accommodate themselves to vision at different distances, without consciousness on our part. The highest specializations of this kind of nerve-function are displayed by the ant and the bee; their wonderful instinctive acts show to what a degree of special perfection sensori-motor action may be brought.[1]

[1] I do not say that the ant and the bee are entirely destitute of any power of adaptation to new experiences in their lives—that they are, in fact, purely organized machines, acting always with unvarying regularity; it would appear, indeed, from close observation, that these creatures do sometimes discover in their actions traces of a sensibility to strange experiences, and of corresponding adaptation of movements. We cannot, moreover, conceive how the remarkable in-

Unlike the bee and the ant, man must slowly learn the use of his senses and their respondent movements. This he does by virtue of the fundamental property of nerve-centres, whereby they react in a definite way to suitable impressions, organically register their experience, and so acquire by education their special faculties. Thus it is that many of the daily actions of our life, which directly follow impressions on the senses, take place in answer to sensations that are not perceived—become, so to speak, *instinctive;* some of them being not a whit less automatic than the instinctive acts of the bee, or the acts of the pigeon deprived of its hemispheres. When we move about in a room with the objects in which we are quite familiar, we direct our steps so as to avoid them, without being conscious what they are, or what we are doing; we *see* them, as we easily discover if we try to move about in the same way with our eyes shut, but we

stincts which they manifest can have been acquired originally, except by virtue of some such power. But the power in them now is evidently of a rudimentary kind, and must remain so while they have not those higher nerve-centres in which the sensations are combined into ideas, and perceptions of the relations of things are acquired. Granting, however, that the bee or ant has these traces of adaptive action, it must be allowed that they are truly rudiments of functions, which in the supreme nerve-centres we designate as reason and volition. Such a confession might be a trouble to a metaphysical physiologist, who would thereupon find it necessary to place a metaphysical entity behind the so-called instincts of the bee, but can be no trouble to the inductive physiologist; he simply recognizes an illustration of a physiological diffusion of properties, and of the physical conditions of primitive volition, and traces in the evolution of mind and its organs, as in the evolution of other functions and their organs, a progressive specialization and increasing complexity.

do not *perceive* them, the mind being fully occupied with
some train of thought.   In like manner, when we go
through a series of familiar acts, as in dressing or un-
dressing ourselves, the operations are really automatic ;
once begun, we continue them in a mechanical order,
while the mind is thinking of other things ; and if we
afterwards reflect upon what we have done, in order to
call to mind whether we did or did not omit something,
as for instance to wind up our watch, we cannot satisfy
ourselves except by trial, even though we had actually
done what we were in doubt about.   It is evident,
indeed, that in a state of profound reverie or abstraction
a person may, as a somnambulist sometimes does, see
without knowing that he sees, hear without knowing that
he hears, and go through a series of acts scarcely, if at
all, conscious of them at the time, and not remembering them afterwards.   For the most distinct display of
sensori-motor action in man, it is necessary that his cerebral hemispheres, which are so largely developed, and
intervene much in the functions of the subordinate
centres, should be deeply engaged in their own functions,
or that these should be suspended.   This appears to be
the case in those brief attacks of epileptic unconscious-
ness known as the *petit mal*, in which a person will
sometimes go on with the work he was engaged in at the
time of the attack, utterly unaware of the momentary
interruption of his consciousness.[1]   There are many
instances of this sort on record, which I cannot stop to

[1] For examples I may refer to my work on *The Physiology and
Pathology of Mind*, 2nd Edition.

relate now; they prove how large a part sensori-motor functions, which are the highest nerve functions of so many animals, play in our daily actions. We ought clearly to apprehend the fact that, as with the spinal cord, so here, the movements which take place in answer to the stimulus from without may be excited by the stimulus of the will descending from the hemispheres, and that, when they are so excited, the immediate agency of them is the same. The movements that are out-wardly manifest are, as it were, contained inwardly in the appropriate motor nuclei; these have been educated to perform them. Hence it is that, when the left corpus striatum is broken up by disease, the right cannot do its special work; if it could, a man might write with his left hand when his right hand was dis-abled by paralysis.

Thus much, then, concerning our sensori-motor acts. When we have yielded up to the spinal cord all the part in our actions that properly belongs to it, and to the sensory ganglia and their connected motor nuclei all the part that belongs to them, we have subtracted no incon-siderable part from the phenomena which we are in the habit of designating mental and including under mind. But we still leave untouched the highest functions of the nervous system—those to which the hemispherical ganglia minister. These are the functions of intelligence, of emotion, and of will; they are the strictly mental functions. The question at once arises whether we have to do in these supreme centres with fundamentally different properties and different laws of evolution from

c

those which belong to the lower nerve-centres. We have to do with different functions certainly; but are the organic processes which take place in them essentially different from, or are they identical with, those of the lower nerve-ecntres ? They appear to be essentially the same : there is a reception of impressions, and there is a reaction to impressions, and there is an organic registration of the effects both of the impressions and of the reactions to them. The external stimuli do not, it is true, ascend directly to the supreme centres as they do to the spinal centres and the sensory centres ; they are transmitted indirectly through the sensory ganglia ; it is through the senses that we get our ideas. This is in accordance with the anatomical observation—which, however, is disputed—that no sensory fibres go directly through to the hemispheres, and no motor fibres start directly from them ; both sensory and motor fibres stopping at the corpora striata and thalami optici, and new fibres connecting these with the hemispheres. But this does not alter the fundamental similarity of the organic processes in the higher centres. The impressions which are made there are the physiological conditions of *ideas ;* the feeling of the ideas is *emotion*—for I hold emotion to mean the special sensibility of the vesicular neurine to ideas ;—the registration of them is *memory ;* and the reaction to them is *volition. Attention* is the maintenance of the tension of an idea or a group of ideas—the keeping it before the mind; and *reflection* is the successive transference of energy from one to another of a series of ideas. We know not, and perhaps never shall know,

what mind is; but we are nevertheless bound to investigate, in a scientific spirit, the laws of its functions,
and to trace the resemblances which undoubtedly
exist between them and the functions of lower nerve-
centres.

Take, for example, the so-called faculty of memory, of
which metaphysicians have made so much as affording
us the knowledge of personal identity. From the way
in which they usually treat of it, one would suppose that
memory was peculiar to mind, and far beyond the reach
of physical explanation. But a little reflection will prove
that it is nothing of the kind. The acquired functions
of the spinal cord, and of the sensory ganglia, obviously
imply the existence of memory, which is indispensable
to their formation and exercise. How else could these
centres be educated? The impressions made upon
them, and the answering movements, both leave their
traces behind them, which are capable of being revived
on the occasions of similar impressions. A ganglionic
centre, whether of mind, sensation, or movement, which
was without memory, would be an idiotic centre, incapable of being taught its functions. In every nerve-cell
there is memory, and not only so, but there is memory
in every organic element of the body. The virus of
small-pox or of syphilis makes its mark on the constitution for the rest of life. We may forget it, but it will
not forget us, though, like the memory of an old man, it
may fade and become faint with advancing age. The
manner in which the scar of a cut in a child's finger is
perpetuated, and grows as the body grows, evinces, as

Mr. Paget has pointed out, that the organic element of the part remembers the change which it has suffered. Memory is the organic registration of the effects of impressions, the organization of experience, and to recollect is to revive this experience—to call the organized residua into functional activity.

The fact that memory is accompanied by consciousness in the supreme centres does not alter the fundamental nature of the organic processes that are the condition of it. The more sure and perfect, indeed, memory becomes, the more unconscious it becomes; and when an idea or mental state has been completely organized, it is revived without consciousness, and takes its part automatically in our mental operations, just as a habitual movement does in our bodily activity. We perceive in operation here the same law of organization of conscious acquisitions as unconscious power, which we observed in the functions of the lower nerve-centres. A child, while learning to speak or read, has to remember the meaning of each word, must tediously exercise its memory; but which of us finds it necessary to remember the meanings of the common words which we are daily using, as we must do those of a foreign language with which we are not very familiar? We do remember them, of course, but it is by an unconscious memory. In like manner, a pupil, learning to play the pianoforte, is obliged to call to mind each note : but the skilful player goes through no such process of conscious remembrance ; his ideas, like his movements, are automatic, and both so rapid as to surpass the rapidity of succession of conscious ideas and movements. To my mind, there are incontrovertible reasons to conclude that the organic conditions of memory are the same in the supreme centres of thought as they are in the lower centres of sensation and of reflex action. Accordingly, in a brain that is not disorganized by injury or disease, the organic registrations are never actually forgotten, but endure while life lasts ; no wave of oblivion can efface their characters. Consciousness, it is true, may be impotent to recall them ; but a fever, a blow on the head, a poison in the blood, a dream, the agony of drowning, the hour of death, rending the veil between our present consciousness and these inscriptions, will sometimes call vividly back, in a momentary flash, and call back too with all the feelings of the original experience, much that seemed to have vanished from the mind for ever. In the deepest and most secret recesses of mind, there is nothing hidden from the individual self, or from others, which may not be thus some time accidentally revealed ; so that it might well be that, as De Quincey surmised, the opening of the book at the day of judgment shall be the unfolding of the everlasting scroll of memory.[1]

As it is with memory so is it with volition, which is a physiological function of the supreme centres, and which, like memory, becomes more unconscious and automatic the more completely it is organized by repeated practice.

---

[1] An apt illustration, most true to nature, of the recurrence of early impressions in the delirium of dying, is afforded by Falstaff, who, as he expires in a London tavern after a life of debauchery, babbles of green fields.

It is not man's function in life to think and feel only;
his inner life he must express or utter in action of some
kind—in word or deed. Receiving the impressions from
nature, of which he is a part, he reacts upon nature
intelligently, modifying it in a variety of ways; thus
nature passes through human nature to a higher evolution.
As the spinal cord reacts to its impressions in excito-
motor action, and as the sensory centres react to their
impressions in sensori-motor action, so, after the complex
interworking and combination of ideas in the hemispherical ganglia, there is, in like manner, a reaction or desire
of determination of energy outwards, in accordance with
the fundamental property of organic structure to seek
what is beneficial and shun what is hurtful to it. It is
this property of tissue that gives the impulse which, when
guided by intelligence, we call volition, and it is the
abstraction from the particular volitions which metaphysicians personify as *the will*, and regard as their
determining agent. Physiologically, we cannot choose
but reject *the* will : volition we know, and will we know,
but *the will*, apart from particular acts of volition or will,
we cannot know. To interpose such a metaphysical
entity between reflection and action thereupon, would
bring us logically to the necessity of interposing a similar
entity between the stimulus to the spinal cord and its reaction. Thus, instead of unravelling the complex by help
of the more simple, we should obscure the simple by
speculations concerning the complex. As physiologists
we have to deal with volition as a function of the supreme
centres, following reflection, varying in quantity and

quality as its cause varies, strengthened by education and exercise, enfeebled by disuse, decaying with decay of structure, and always needing for its outward expression the educated agency of the subordinate motor centres. We have to deal with will, not as a single undecomposable faculty unaffected by bodily conditions, but as a result of organic changes in the supreme centres, affected as certainly and seriously by disorder of them as our motor faculties are by disorder of their centres.   Loss of power of will is one of the earliest and most characteristic symptoms of mental derangement ; and, whatever may have been thought in times past, we know well now that the loss is not the work of some unclean spirit that has laid its hands upon the will, but the direct effect of physical disease.

But I must pass on now to other matters, without stopping to unfold at length the resemblances between the properties of the supreme centres and those of the lower nerve-centres.   We see that the supreme centres are educated, as the other centres are, and the better they are educated the better do they perform their functions of thinking and willing.   The development of mind is a gradual process of organization in them.   Ideas, as they are successively acquired through the gateways of the senses, are blended and combined and grouped in a complexity that defies analysis, the organic combinations being the physiological conditions of our highest mental operations—reflection, reasoning, and judgment.   Two leading ideas we ought to grasp and hold fast : first, that the complex and more recondite phenomena of mind are formed out of the more simple and elementary by progressive specialization and integration ; and, secondly, that the laws by means of which this formation takes place are not laws of association merely, but laws of organic combination and evolution. The growth of mental power means an actual addition of structure to the intimate constitution of the centres of mind—a *mental organization* in them ; and mental derangement means disorder of them, primary or secondary, functional or organic.

Although I have declared the hemispherical ganglia to be pre-eminently the mind-centres, and although it is in disorder of their functions—in disordered intelligence, in disordered emotion, and in disordered will—that insanity essentially consists, it is nevertheless impossible to limit the study of our mental operations to the study of them. They receive impressions from every part of the body, and, there is reason to believe, exert an influence on every element of it : there is not an organic motion, sensible or insensible, which does not, consciously or unconsciously, affect them, and which they in turn do not consciously or unconsciously affect. So intimate and essential is the sympathy between all the organic functions, of which mind is the crown and consummation, that we may justly say of it, that it sums up and comprehends the bodily life—that everything which is displayed outwardly is contained secretly in the innermost. We cannot truly understand mind functions without embracing in our inquiry all the bodily functions and, I might perhaps without exaggeration say, all the bodily features.

I have already shown this in respect of motor functions, by exhibiting how entirely dependent for its expression will is upon the organized mechanism of the motor centres—how, in effecting voluntary movements, it presupposes the appropriate education of the motor centres. Few persons, perhaps, consider what a wonderful art speech is, or even remember that it is an art which we acquire. But it actually costs us a great deal of pains to learn to speak ; all the language which an infant has is a cry ; and it is only because we begin to learn to talk when we are very young, and are constantly practising, that we forget how specially we have had to educate our motor centres of speech. Here, however, we come to another pregnant consideration : the acquired faculty of the educated motor centre is not only a necessary agency in the performance of a voluntary act, but I maintain that it positively enters as a mental element into the composition of the definite volition ; that, in fact, the specific motor faculty not only acts downwards upon the motor nerves, thus executing the movement, but also acts upwards upon the mind-centres, thereby giving to consciousness the conception of the suitable movement— the appropriate motor intuition. It is certain that, in order to execute consciously a voluntary act, we must have in the mind a conception of the aim or purpose of the act. The will cannot act upon the separate muscles, it can only determine the result desired ; and thereupon the combined contraction, in due force and rapidity, of the separate muscles takes place in a way that we have no consciousness of, and accomplishes the act. The

infant directly it is born can suck, certainly not consciously or voluntarily; on the first occasion, at any rate,
it can have no notion of the purpose of its movements;
but the effect of the action is to excite in the mind the
special motor intuition, and to lay the foundation of the
special volition of it. We cannot do an act voluntarily
unless we know what we are going to do, and we cannot
know exactly what we are going to do until we have
taught ourselves to do it. This exact knowledge of the
aim of the act, which we get by experience, the motor
intuition gives us.

The essential intervention of the motor intuition, which
is, as it were, the abstract of the movement, in our
mental life, is best illustrated by the movements of speech,
but is by no means peculiar to them. Each word represents a certain association and succession of muscular
acts, and is itself nothing more than a conventional
sign or symbol to mark the particular muscular expression
of a particular idea. The word has not independent
vitality; it differs in different languages; and those who
are deprived of the power of articulate speech must make
use of other muscular acts to express their ideas, speaking,
as it were, in a dumb discourse. There is no reason on
earth, indeed, why a person might not learn to express
every thought which he can utter in speech by movements of his fingers, limbs, and body—by the silent
language of gesture. The movements of articulation
have not, then, a special *kind* of connection with the mind,
though their connection is a specially intimate one; they
are simply the most convenient for the expression of our

mental states, because they are so numerous, various, delicate, and complex, and because, in conjunction with the muscles of the larynx and the respiratory muscles, they modify sound, and thus make audible language. Having, on this account, been always used as the special instruments of utterance, their connection with thought is most intimate; the Greeks, in fact, used the word λόγος to mean both reason and speech. But this does not make the relations of the movements of speech to mind different fundamentally from the relations of other voluntary movements to mind; and we should be quite as much warranted in assigning to the mind a special faculty of writing, of walking, or of gesticulating, as in speaking of a special faculty of speech in it.

What is true of the relations of articulate movements to mental states is true of the relations of other movements to mental states : they not only express the thought, but, when otherwise put in action, they can excite the appropriate thought. Speak the word, and the idea of which it is the expression is aroused, though it was not in the mind previously; or put other muscles than those of speech into an attitude which is the normal expression of a certain mental state, and the latter is excited. Most if not all men, when thinking, repeat internally, whisper to themselves, as it were, what they are thinking about; and persons of dull and feeble intelligence cannot comprehend what they read, or what is sometimes said to them, without calling the actual movement to their aid, and repeating the words in a whisper or aloud. As speech has become the almost exclusive mode of expressing our thoughts, there not being many gestures of the body which are the habitual expressions of simple ideas, we cannot present striking examples of the powers of other movements to call up the appropriate ideas; yet the delicate muscular adaptations which effect the accommodation of the eye to vision at different distances seem really to give to the mind its ideas of distance and magnitude. No one actually sees distance and magnitude; he sees only certain signs from which he has learned to judge intuitively of them—the muscular adaptations, though he is unconscious of them, imparting the suitable intuitions.

The case is stronger, however, in regard to our emotions. Visible muscular expression is to passion what language or audible muscular expression is to thought. Bacon rightly, therefore, pointed out the advantage of a study of the forms of expression. " For," he says, " the lineaments of the body do disclose the disposition and inclination of the mind in general ; but the motions of the countenance and parts do not only so, but do further disclose the present humour and state of the mind or will." The muscles of the countenance are the chief exponents of human feeling, much of the variety of which is due to the action of the orbicular muscles with the system of elevating and depressing muscles. Animals cannot laugh, because, besides being incapable of ludicrous ideas, they do not possess in sufficient development the orbicular muscle of the lips and the straight muscles which act upon them. It is because of the superadded muscles and of their combined actions—not combined contraction merely, but con-

sentaneous action, the relaxation of some accompanying
the contraction of others—that the human countenance
is capable of expressing a variety of more complex
emotions than animals can. Those who would degrade
the body, in order, as they imagine, to exalt the mind,
should consider more deeply than they do the importance
of our muscular expressions of feeling. The manifold
shades and kinds of expression which the lips present—
their gibes, gambols, and flashes of merriment ; the quick
language of a quivering nostril ; the varied waves and
ripples of beautiful emotion which play on the human
countenance, with the spasms of passion that disfigure it—
all which we take such pains to embody in art,—are
simply effects of muscular action, and might be produced
by electricity or any other stimulus, if we could only
apply it in suitable force to the proper muscles. When
the eye is turned upwards in rapt devotion, in the ecstasy
of supplication, it is for the same reason as it is rolled
upwards in fainting, in sleep, in the agony of death : it
is an involuntary act of the oblique muscles, when the
straight muscles cease to act upon it. We perceive, then,
in the study of muscular action the reason why man looks
up to heaven in prayer, and why he has placed there the
power "whence cometh his help." A simple property of
the body, as Sir C. Bell observes—the fact that the eye
in supplication takes what is its natural position when
not acted upon by the will—has influenced our conceptions of heaven, our religious observances, and the
habitual expression of our highest feelings.

Whether each passion which is special in kind has its

special bodily expression, and what is the expression of
each, it would take me too long to examine now. Suffice
it to say that the special muscular action is not merely the
exponent of the passion, but truly an essential part of it.
Fix the countenance in the pattern of a particular emotion
—in a look of anger, of wonder, or of scorn,—and the
emotion whose appearance is thus imitated will not fail
to be aroused.   And if we try, while the features are
fixed in the expression of one passion, to call up in the
mind a quite different one, we shall find it impossible to
do so.   This agrees with the experiments of Mr. Braid
on persons whom he had put into a state of hypnotism ;
for when the features or the limbs were made by him to
assume the expression of a particular emotion, thereupon
the emotion was actually felt by the patient, who began
to act as if he was under its influence. We perceive then
that the muscles are not alone the machinery by which
the mind acts upon the world, but that their actions are
essential elements in our mental operations.   The superiority of the human over the animal mind seems to be
essentially connected with the greater variety of muscular
action of which man is capable : were he deprived of the
infinitely varied movements of hands, tongue, larynx,
lips, and face, in which he is so far ahead of the animals,
it is probable that he would be no better than an idiot,
notwithstanding he might have a normal development
of brain.[1]

---

[1] There may be no little truth, therefore, though not the entire
truth, in the saying of Anaxagoras, that man is the wisest of animals
by reason of his having hands.

If these reflections are well grounded, it is obvious that disorder of the motor centres may have, as I believe it has, no little effect upon the phenomena of mental derangement. In some cases of insanity there are genuine muscular hallucinations, just as there are in dreams sometimes, when the muscles are in a constrained attitude ; and where the morbid effects are not so marked, there is good reason to suppose that a searching inquiry along this almost untrodden path will disclose the mode of generation of many delusions that seem now inexplicable.

But we cannot limit a complete study of mind even by a full knowledge of the functions of the nervous and muscular systems. The organic system has most certainly an essential part in the constitution and the functions of mind. In the great mental revolution caused by the development of the sexual system at puberty we have the most striking example of the intimate and essential sympathy between the brain as a mental organ and other organs of the body. The change of character at this period is not by any means limited to the appearance of the sexual feelings and their sympathetic ideas, but, when traced to its ultimate reach, will be found to extend to the highest feelings of mankind, social, moral, and even religious. In its lowest sphere, as a mere animal instinct, it is clear that the sexual appetite forces the most selfish person out of the little circle of self-feeling into a wider feeling of family sympathy and a rudimentary moral feeling. The consequence is that, when an individual is sexually mutilated at an early age, he is emasculated morally as well as physically. Eunuchs are said to be the most depraved creatures morally : they are cowardly, envious, liars, utterly deceitful, and destitute of real social feeling.   And there is certainly a characteristic variety of insanity caused by self-abuse, which makes the patient very like a eunuch in character.

It has been affirmed by some philosophers that there is no essential difference between the mind of a woman and that of a man ; and that if a girl were subjected to the same education as a boy, she would resemble him in tastes, feelings, pursuits, and powers.   To my mind it would not be one whit more absurd to affirm that the antlers of the stag, the human beard, and the cock's comb are effects of education ; or that, by putting a girl to the same education as a boy, the female generative organs might be trans-formed into male organs.   The physical and mental differ-ences between the sexes intimate themselves very early in life, and declare themselves most distinctly at puberty : they are connected with the influence of the organs of generation.   The forms and habits of mutilated men ap-proach those of women ; and women whose ovaries and uterus remain from some cause in a state of complete inaction, approach the forms and habits of men.   It is said, too, that in hermaphrodites the mental character, like the physical, participates equally in that of both sexes.   While woman preserves her sex, she will neces-sarily be feebler than man, and, having her special bodily and mental characters, will have to a certain extent her own sphere of activity ; where she has become thoroughly masculine in nature, or hermaphrodite in mind,—when, in fact, she has pretty well divested herself of her sex,—then she may take his ground, and do his work ; but she will have lost her feminine attractions, and probably also her chief feminine functions.

Allowing that the generative organs have their specific effect upon the mind, the question occurs whether each of the internal organs has not also a special effect, giving rise to particular feelings with their sympathetic ideas. They are notably united in the closest sympathy, so that, although insensible to touch, they have a sensibility of their own, by virtue of which they agree in a consent of functions, and respond more or less to one another's sufferings ; and there can be no question that the brain, as the leading member of this physiological union, is sensible of, and affected by, the conditions of its fellow-members. We have not the same opportunity of observing the specific effects of other organs that we have in the case of the generative organs ; for while those come into functional action directly after birth, these come into action abruptly at a certain period, and thus exhibit their specific effects in a decided manner. It may well be, however, that the general uniformity among men in their passions and emotions is due to the specific sympathies of organs, just as the uniformity of their ideas of external nature is due to the uniform operation of the organs of sense.

It is probable that an exact observation of the mental effects of morbid states of the different organs would help the inquiry into the feelings and desires of the mind which owe their origin to particular organs.

What are the psychological features of disease of the
heart, disease of the lungs, disease of the liver? They
are unquestionably different in each case. The inquiry,
which has never yet been seriously attempted, is,
without doubt, a difficult one, but I believe that the
phenomena of dreams might, if carefully observed,
afford some help. The ground-tone of feeling in a
dream, the background on which the phantoms move,
is often determined by the state of an internal organ,
the irritation of which awakens into some degree of
activity that part of the brain with which the organ
is in specific sympathy; accordingly sympathetic ideas
spring out of the feeling and unite in a more or less
coherent dream drama. How plainly this happens in
the case of the generative organs it is unnecessary to
point out: exciting their specific dreams, they teach
a lesson concerning physiological sympathies which,
applied to the observation of the effects of other
organs, may be largely useful in the interpretation, not
of dreams only, but of the phenomena of insanity.
Dreams furnish a particularly fruitful field for the study
of the specific effects of organs on mind, because
these effects are more distinctly felt and more distinctly
declared when the impressions from the external senses
are shut out by sleep. As the stars are not visible,
although they still shine, in the daytime, so the effects
of an internal organ may not be perceptible during the
walking state while consciousness is actively engaged.
But just as, when the sun goes down, the stars shine
visibly, which before were invisible, veiled by his greater

light, so when active consciousness is suspended, organic sympathies, which before were insensible, declare themselves in the mind. Perhaps it is in the excitation of its sympathetic feeling and ideas by a disordered organ during sleep that we may discover the explanation of a fact which seems to be undoubted, and to be more than accidental—namely, that a person has sometimes dreamed prophetically that he would have a particular internal disease, before he consciously felt a symptom of it, and has been afterwards surprised to find his dream come true.

It is natural to suppose that the passion which a particular organ produces in the mind will be that which, when otherwise excited, discharges itself specially upon that organ. Notably this is the case with the sexual organs and the passion to which they minister. When we consider the effects which a joyful anticipation, or the elation of a present excitement, has upon the lungs—the accelerated breathing and the general bodily exhilaration which it occasions—we cannot help thinking of the strange hopefulness and the sanguine expectations of the consumptive patient, who, on the edge of the grave, projects, without a shadow of distrust, what he will do long after he will have been "green in death and festering in his shroud." Observe how fear strikes the heart, and what anxious fear and apprehension accompany some affections of the heart. Anger, disappointment, and envy notably touch the liver; which, in its turn, when deranged, engenders a gloomy tone of mind through which all things have a malignant look,

and from which, when philosophy avails not to free
us, the restoration of its functions will yield instant
relief. The internal organs are plainly not the agents
of their special functions only, but, by reason of the
intimate consent or sympathy of functions, they are
essential constituents of our mental life.

The time yet at my disposal will not allow me to
do more than mention the effects of mental states
on the intimate processes of nutrition and secretion.
Emotion may undoubtedly favour, hinder, or pervert
nutrition, and increase, lessen, or alter a secretion ; in
doing which there is reason to think that it acts, not
only by dilating or contracting the vessels through the
vaso-motor system, as we witness in the blush of shame
and the pallor of fear, but also directly on the organic
elements of the part through the nerves, which, as the
latest researches seem to show, end in them sometimes
by continuity of substance. If they do so end, it is
difficult to conceive how a strong emotion vibrating
to the ultimate fibrils of a nerve can fail to affect for a
moment or longer the functions of the organic elements.
Be this so or not, however, the familiar observations—
first, that a lively hope or joy exerts an enlivening effect
upon the bodily life, quiet and equable when moderate,
but, when stronger, evinced in the brilliancy of the
eve, in the quickened pulse and respiration, in an
inclination to laugh and sing ; and, secondly, that grief
or other depressing passion has an opposite effect, re-
laxing the arteries, enfeebling the heart, making the eye
dull, impeding digestion, and producing an inclination to

sigh and weep,—these familiar observations of opposite
effects indicate the large part which mental states may
play, not in the causation of all sorts of disease alone,
but in aiding recovery from them. A sudden and
great mental shock may, like a great physical shock,
and perhaps in the same way, paralyse for a time all the
bodily and mental functions, or cause instant death.
It may, again, produce epilepsy, apoplexy, or insanity;
while a prolonged state of depression and anxiety is
sometimes an important agent in the causation of
chronic disease, such as diabetes and heart-disease.
Can it be doubted, too, that the strong belief that a
bodily disorder will be cured by some appliance, itself
innocent of good or harm, may so affect beneficially
the nutrition of the part as actually to effect a cure?
To me it seems not unreasonable to suppose that the
mind may stamp its tone, if not its very features, on
the individual elements of the body, inspiring them
with hope and energy, or infecting them with despair
and feebleness. A separated portion of the body, so
little that our naked eye can make nothing of it, the
spermatozoon of the male and the ovum of the female,
does at any rate contain, in a latent state, the essential
characters of the mind and body of the individual from
whom it has proceeded; and as we are utterly ignorant
how this mysterious effect is accomplished, we are certainly
not in a position to deny that what is true of the spermatozoon and ovum may be true of other organic elements.
And if this be so, then those who profess to discover
the character of the individual in the character of the

nose, the hand, the features, or other part of the body, may have a foundation of truth for speculations which are yet only vague, fanciful, and valueless.

Perhaps we do not, as physicians, consider sufficiently the influence of mental states in the production of disease, and their importance as symptoms, or take all the advantage which we might take of them in our efforts to cure it. Quackery seems to have here got hold of a truth which legitimate medicine fails to appreciate and use adequately. Assuredly the most successful physician is he who, inspiring the greatest confidence in his remedies, strengthens and exalts the imagination of his patient: if he orders a few drops of peppermint-water with the confident air of curing the disease, will he not really do more sometimes for the patient than one who treats him in the most approved scientific way, but without inspiring a conviction of recovery? Ceremonies, charms, gesticulations, amulets, and the like, have in all ages and among all nations been greatly esteemed and largely used in the treatment of disease; and it may be speciously presumed that they have derived their power, not from any contract with the supernatural, but, as Bacon observes, by strengthening and exalting the imagination of him who used them. Entirely ignorant as we are, and probably ever shall be, of the nature of mind, groping feebly for the laws of its operation, we certainly cannot venture to set bounds to its power over those intimate and insensible molecular movements which are the basis of all our visible bodily functions, any more than we can justly venture to set bounds to its action in the vast and ever-progressing evolution of nature, of which all our thoughts and works are but a part. This much we do know: that as, on the one hand, in the macrocosm of nature, it is certain that the true idea once evolved is imperishable—that it passes from individual to individual, from nation to nation, from generation to generation, becoming the eternal and exalting possession of man; so, on the other hand, in the microcosm of the body, which some ignorantly despise, there are many more things in the reciprocal action of mind and organic element than are yet dreamt of in our philosophy.

LECTURE II.

GENTLEMEN,—In my last lecture I gave a general survey of the physiology of our mental functions, showing how indissolubly they are bound up with the bodily functions, and how barren must of necessity be a study of mind apart from body. I pointed out that the higher mental operations were functions of the supreme nerve-centres; but that, though of a higher and more complex nature than the functions of the lower nerve-centres, they obeyed the same physiological laws of evolution, and could be best approached through a knowledge of them. I now propose to show that the phenomena of the derangement of mind bear out fully this view of its nature; that we have not to deal with disease of a metaphysical entity, which the method of inductive inquiry cannot reach, nor the resources of the medical art touch, but with disease of the nervous system, disclosing itself by physical and mental symptoms. I say advisedly physical and mental, because in most, if not all, cases of insanity, at one period or other of their course, there are, in addition to the prominent mental features, symptoms of disordered nutrition and secretion, of disordered sensibility, or of disordered motility. Neither in health nor in disease is the mind imprisoned in one corner of the body; and when a person is lunatic, he is, as Dr. Bucknill has remarked, lunatic to his fingers' ends.

Mental disorders are neither more nor less than nervous diseases in which mental symptoms predominate, and their entire separation from other nervous diseases has been a sad hindrance to progress. When a blow on the head has paralysed sensibility and movement, in consequence of the disease in the brain which it has initiated, the patient is sent to the hospital; but when a blow on the head has caused mental derangement, in consequence of the disease of brain which it has initiated, the patient is sent to an asylum. In like manner, one man who has unluckily swallowed the eggs of a tænia, and has got a cysticercus in the brain, may go to the hospital; another who has been similarly unlucky goes to an asylum. Syphilitic disease of the brain or its arteries lands one person in an asylum with mental symptoms predominant, another in an hospital with sensory and motor disorder predominant. The same cause produces different symptoms, according to the part of the brain which it particularly affects. No doubt it is right that mental derangements should have, as they often require, the special appliances of an asylum, but it is certainly not right that the separation which is necessary for treatment should reach to their pathology and to the method of its study. So long as this is the case, we shall labour in vain to get exact scientific ideas concerning their causation, their pathology, and their treatment.

Clearing, then, the question as completely as possible from the haze which metaphysics has cast around it, let us ask—How comes idiocy, or insanity? What is the scientific meaning of them? We may take it to be beyond question that they are not accidents ; that they come to pass, as every other event in nature does, by natural law. They are mysterious visitations only because we understand not the laws of their production, appear casualties only because we are ignorant of their causality. When a blow on the head or an inflammation of the membranes of the brain has produced derangement of mind, we need not look farther for a cause : the actual harm done to structure is sufficient to account for disorder of function in the best-constituted and best-developed brain. But it is only in a small proportion of cases of insanity that we can discover such a direct physical occasion of disease. In a great many cases—in more than half, certainly, and perhaps in five out of six—there is something in the nervous organization of the person, some native peculiarity, which, however we name it, pre-disposes him to an outbreak of insanity. When two persons undergo a similar moral shock, or a similar prolonged anxiety, and one of them goes mad in consequence, while the other goes to sleep and goes to work and recovers his equanimity, it is plain that all the co-operating conditions have not been the same, that the entire cause has been different. What, then, has been the difference? In the former case there has been

present a most important element, which was happily
wanting in the latter—there has been a certain hereditary neurosis, an unknown and variable quantity in the
equation.

Perhaps of all the erroneous notions concerning mind
which metaphysics has engendered or abetted, there is
none more false than that which tacitly assumes or
explicitly declares that men are born with equal original
mental capacity, opportunities and education determining
the differences of subsequent development. The opinion
is as cruel as it is false. What man can by taking thought
add one cubit either to his mental or to his bodily
stature? Multitudes of human beings come into the
world weighted with a destiny against which they have
neither the will nor the power to contend; they are the
step-children of nature, and groan under the worst of
all tyrannies—the tyranny of a bad organization. Men
differ, indeed, in the fundamental characters of their
minds, as they do in the features of their countenances,
or in the habits of their bodies; and between those who
are born with the potentiality of a full and complete
mental development, under favourable circumstances, and
those who are born with an innate incapacity of mental
development, under any circumstances, there exists every
gradation. What teaching could ever raise the congenital
idiot to the common level of human intelligence? What
teaching could ever keep the inspired mind of the man
of genius at that level?

The congenital idiot is deprived of his human birth-
right; for he is born with such a defect of brain that he

cannot display any, or can only display very feeble and imperfect mental functions. From no fault of his own is he thus afflicted, seeing that he must be held innocent of all offence but the offence of his share of original sin ; but it is nowise so clear that it is not from some fault of his parents. It is all too true that, in many cases, there has observably been a neglect or disregard of the laws which govern the progress of human development through the ages. Idiocy is, indeed, a manufactured article ; and although we are not always able to tell how it is manufactured, still its important causes are known and are within control. Many cases are distinctly traceable to parental intemperance and excess. Out of 300 idiots in Massachusetts, Dr. Howe found as many as 145 to be the offspring of intemperate parents ; and there are numerous scattered observations which prove that chronic alcoholism in the parent may directly occasion idiocy in the child. I think, too, that there is no reasonable question of the ill effects of marriages of consanguinity : that their tendency is to produce degeneracy of the race, and idiocy as the extremest form of such degeneracy. I do not say that *all* the children of such marriages may not sometimes be healthy, and *some* of them quite healthy at other times ; but the general and ultimate result of breeding in and in is to produce barrenness and sterility, children of a low degree of viability and of imperfect mental and physical development, deaf-mutism, and actual imbecility or idiocy. Again, insanity in the parent may issue in idiocy in the offspring, which is, so to speak, the natural term of mental degeneracy when it goes on unchecked through generations. It may be affirmed with no little confidence, that if the experiment of inter-marrying insane persons for two or three generations were tried, the result would be sterile idiocy and extinction of the family. Certain unfavourable conditions of life tend unquestionably to produce degeneracy of the individual; the morbid predisposition so generated is then trans-mitted to the next generation, and, if the unfavourable conditions continue, is aggravated in it; and thus is formed a morbid variety of the human kind, which is incapable of being a link in the line of progress of humanity. Nature puts it under the ban of sterility, and thus prevents the permanent degradation of the race. Morel has traced through four generations the family history of a youth who was admitted into the asylum at Rouen in a state of stupidity and semi-idiocy; the sum-mary of which may fitly illustrate the natural course of degeneracy when it goes on through generations.

First generation: Immorality, depravity, alcoholic excess and moral degradation, in the great-grandfather, who was killed in a tavern brawl.

Second generation: Hereditary drunkenness, mania-cal attacks, ending in general paralysis, in the grandfather.

Third generation: Sobriety, but hypochondriacal ten-dencies, delusions of persecutions, and homicidal tenden-cies in the father.

Fourth generation: Defective intelligence. First attack of mania at sixteen; stupidity, and transition to complete idiocy. Furthermore probable extinction of the family; for the generative functions were as little developed as those of a child of twelve years of age. He had two sisters who were both defective physically and morally, and were classed as imbeciles. To complete the proof of heredity in this case Morel adds, that the mother had a child while the father was confined in the asylum, and that this adulterous child showed no signs of degeneracy.

When epilepsy in young children leads to idiocy, as it often does, we must generally look for the deep root of the mischief in the family neurosis.

No one can well dispute that in the case of such an extreme morbid variety as a congenital idiot is, we have to do with a defective nervous organization. We are still, however, without more than a very few exact descriptions of the brains of idiots. Mr. Marshall has recently examined and described the brains of two idiots of European descent. He found the convolutions to be fewer in number, individually less complex, broader and smoother than in the apes: "in this respect," he says, "the idiots' brains are even more simple than that of the gibbon, and approach that of the baboon." The condition was the result neither of atrophy nor of mere arrest of growth, but consisted essentially in an imperfect evolution of the cerebral hemispheres or their parts, dependent on an arrest of development. The proportion of the weight of brain to that of body was extraordinarily diminished. We learn, then, that when man is born with a brain no higher—indeed lower—than that of an ape, he may have the convolutions fewer in number, and individually less complex, than they are in the brain of a

chimpanzee and an orang; the human brain may revert
to, or fall below, that type of development from which,
if the theory of Darwin be true, it has gradually ascended
by evolution through the ages.

With the defect of organ there is a corresponding
defect of function. But there is sometimes more than a
simple defect. A curious and interesting fact, which has
by no means yet received the consideration which it
deserves, is that, with the appearance of this animal type
of brain in idiocy, there do sometimes appear or reappear remarkable animal traits and instincts. There is
a class of idiots which may justly be designated *theroid*,
so like brutes are the members of it. The old stories of
so-called wild men, such as Peter the wild boy, and the
young savage of Aveyron, who ran wild in the woods
and lived on acorns and whatever else they could pick
·up there, were certainly exaggerated at the time. These
degraded beings were evidently idiots, who exhibited
a somewhat striking aptitude and capacity for a wild
animal life. Dr. Carpenter, however, quotes the case of
an idiot girl, who was seduced by some miscreant, and
who, when she was delivered, gnawed through the umbilical cord as some of the lower animals do. And Dr.
Crichton Browne, of the West Riding Asylum, records a
somewhat similar case in a young woman, not an idiot
naturally, but who had gone completely demented after
insanity. She had been in the habit of escaping from
home, and of living in solitude in the woods, feeding
upon wild fruits or what she could occasionally beg at a
cottage, and sleeping in the brushwood. She had fre-

quently lived in this manner for a fortnight at a time. During one of these absences she was delivered of twins ; she had sought out a sheltered hollow, and there, reverting to a primitive instinct, gnawed through the umbilical cord. The twins were alive when found two days after birth, but the mother was in a very exhausted state, having had no food or covering since her delivery. "We have at Salpêtrière," says Esquirol, "an imbecile woman, who used to earn a few sous by doing rough household work. It has happened on several occasions that as soon as she got her sous she took them to a labourer, and gave herself up to his brutality ; but when she was pregnant she went no more to him."

In the conformation and habits of other idiots the most careless observer could not help seeing the ape. A striking instance of this kind is described by Dr. Mitchell, Deputy Commissioner in Lunacy for Scotland. "I have never," he says, "seen a better illustration of the ape-faced idiot than in this case. It is not, however, the face alone that is ape-like. He grins, chatters, and screams like a monkey, never attempting a sound in any way resembling a word. He puts himself in the most ape-like attitude in his hunts after lice, and often brings his mouth to help his hands. He grasps what he brings to his mouth with an apish hold. His thumbs are but additional fingers. He has a leaping walk. He has heavy eyebrows, and short hair on his cheek or face. He is muscular, active, and not dwarfish. He sits on the floor in ape fashion, with his genitals always exposed. He has filthy habits of all kinds. He may be called an idiot of the lowest order; yet there is a mischievous brute-like intelligence in his eye. His head is not very small, its greatest circumference being twenty inches and a half, but in shape it strongly exhibits the ape-form of abnormality."

Pinel has recorded the case of an idiot who was something like a sheep, both in respect of her tastes, her mode of life, and the form of her head. She had an aversion to meat, and ate fruit and vegetables greedily, and drank nothing but water. Her demonstrations of sensibility, joy, or trouble, were confined to the repetition of the ill-articulated words, *bé, ma, bah.* She alternately bent and raised her head, and rubbed herself against the belly of the girl who attended her. If she wanted to resist or express her discontent, she tried to butt with the crown of her head; she was very passionate. Her back, her loins, and shoulders were covered with flexible and blackish hairs one or two inches long. She never could be made to sit on a chair or bench, even when at meals; as soon as she was placed in a sitting posture, she glided on the floor. She slept on the floor in the posture of animals.

There is now under care, in the West Riding Asylum, a deformed idiot girl who, in general appearance and habits, has, according to Dr. Browne, striking features of resemblance to a goose; so much so, that the nurses who received her described her as just like "a plucked goose." Her father died in the asylum, and her mother's sister was also a patient in it at one time. She is 4ft. 2in. in height, has a small head, and thin and scanty hair,

E

so that the crown of the head is partially bald. The eyes are large, round, prominent, and restless, and are frequently covered by the eyelids, as if by a slow, forcible effort at winking. The lower jaw is large, projecting more than one inch beyond the contracted upper jaw, and possesses an extraordinary range of antero-posterior, as well as lateral, movement ; the whole configuration of the lower part of the face having a somewhat bill-like appearance. The neck is unusually long and flexible, and is capable of being bent backwards so as actually to touch the back between the scapulæ. The cutis anserina is general over the body, but is most marked on the back and dorsal aspects of the limbs, where it looks exactly as if it had been just deprived of feathers. The inferior angles of the scapulæ stand prominently out, and moving freely with the movements of the arms have precisely the appearance of rudimentary wings. The girl utters no articulate sounds, but expresses pleasure by cackling like a goose, and displeasure by hissing or screeching like a goose, or perhaps like a macaw. When angry, she flaps her arms against her sides, and beats her feet upon the floor. She knows her own name, and understands one or two short sentences, such as " Come here" and " Put out your hand." She recognizes the persons who attend upon her and feed her, and is much agitated if touched by a stranger. She cannot feed herself, but swallows voraciously all that is put into her mouth, showing no preference for one article of diet over another. She is dirty in her habits, and no amount of attention has improved her in this respect. She is very fond of her bath, cackling when she is put into it, and screeching when she is taken out of it.[1]

It is a natural question, Whence come these animal traits and instincts in man? Whence was derived the instinct which taught the idiot woman to gnaw through the umbilical cord? Was it really the reappearance of a primitive instinct of animal nature—a faint echo from a

[1] The following account of an idiot in the Western Counties Idiot Asylum has been communicated to me by Mr. Kenton, surgeon to the Asylum. She is between 15 and 16 years old, has a very small head, but is well formed otherwise, and well nourished. She has little or no intellect, not being able to speak, and barely understanding a few signs. By careful treatment she has been taught to feed herself, but there her education has reached its limit. She has been left to herself, and watched with a view to observe her natural habits. When alone in the garden, she chooses a quiet spot among the shrubs, and, sitting down, will bend forward with her small head between her thighs, and occupy herself in picking imaginary insects from the adjacent parts of her body, pretending to pick them and to throw them away. She will then wander about, and finding a suitable bough, will swing by her hands, and then double her legs over the branch and swing with her head downwards. She will steal anything she fancies, and hide it away; will suddenly spring upon any child near and bite and scratch it, and then in a moment look as demure as if she had done nothing. At certain times she will go under the shrubs, scratch a hole with her hands in the ground, sit down upon it as a cat does, then turn round and carefully cover the spot by scraping the earth over it with her hands. She tears her clothes up into strips, and hides the pieces. Mr. Kenton mentions another idiot under his care, who puts everything to his nose before putting it into his mouth. This he does, not hastily, but deliberately, examining each piece of food carefully by his sense of smell. He greatly dislikes butter, and will not eat pie-crust or any cooked food which contains butter, and he detects its presence with certainty by the sense of smell. He will not kiss anyone till he has sniffed at the person first.

E 2

far distant past, testifying to a kinship which man has
almost outgrown, or has grown too proud to acknowledge?   No doubt such animal traits are marks of
extreme human degeneracy, but it is no explanation to
call them so ; degenerations come by law, and are as
natural as natural law can make them.   Instead of passing them by as abnormal, or, worse still, stigmatizing
them as unnatural, it behoves us to seek for the scientific
interpretation which they must certainly have.   When we
reflect that every human brain does, in the course of its
development, pass through the same stages as the brains
of other vertebrate animals, and that its transitional states
resemble the permanent forms of their brains ; and when
we reflect further, that the stages of its development
in the womb may be considered the abstract and brief
chronicle of a series of developments that have gone on
through countless ages in nature, it does not seem so
wonderful, as at the first blush it might do, that it should,
when in a condition of arrested development, sometimes
display animal instincts.   Summing up, as it were, in
itself the leading forms of the vertebrate type, there is
truly a brute brain within the man's ; and when the latter
stops short of its characteristic development as *human*—
when it remains arrested at or below the level of an
orang's brain, it may be presumed that it will manifest its
most primitive functions, and no higher functions.

I am not aware of any other considerations than those
just adduced which offer even the glimpse of an explanation of the origin of these animal traits in man.   We
need not, however, confine our attention to idiots only.

Whence come the savage snarl, the destructive disposi_
tion, the obscene language, the wild howl, the offensive
habits, displayed by some of the insane? Why should
a human being deprived of his reason ever become so
brutal in character as some do, unless he has the brute
nature within him? In most large asylums there is one,
or more than one, example of a demented person who
truly ruminates : bolting his food rapidly, he retires afterwards to a corner, where at his leisure he quietly brings
it up again into the mouth and masticates it as the cow
does. I should take up a long time if I were to enumerate the various brute-like characteristics that are at times
witnessed among the insane ; enough to say that some
very strong facts and arguments in support of Mr. Darwin's views might be drawn from the field of morbid psychology. We may, without much difficulty, trace savagery
in civilization, as we can trace animalism in savagery ;
and in the degeneration of insanity, in the *unkinding*,
so to say, of the human kind, there are exhibited marks
denoting the elementary instincts of its composition.

It behoves us, as scientific inquirers, to realize distinctly the physical meaning of the progress of human
intelligence from generation to generation. What structural differences in the brain are implied by it? That an
increasing purpose runs through the ages, and that "the
thoughts of men are widened with the process of the suns,"
no one will call in question ; and that this progress has
been accompanied by a progressive development of the
cerebral hemispheres, the convolutions of which have increased in size, number, and complexity, will hardly now

be disputed. Whether the fragments of ancient human crania which have been discovered in Europe do or do not testify to the existence of a barbarous race that disappeared before historical time, they certainly mark a race not higher than the lowest surviving human variety. Dr. Pritchard's comparison of the skulls of the same nation at different periods of its history led him to the conclusion that the present inhabitants of Britain, " either as the result of many ages of great intellectual cultivation or from some other cause, have much more capacious brain-cases than their forefathers." Yet stronger evidence of a growth of brain with the growth of intelligence is furnished by an examination of the brains of existing savages. Gratiolet has figured and described the brain of the Hottentot Venus, who was nowise an idiot. He found a striking simplicity and a regular arrangement of the convolution of the frontal lobes, which presented an almost perfect symmetry in the two hemispheres, involuntarily recalling the regularity and symmetry of the cerebral convolutions in the lower animals. The brain was palpably inferior to that of a normally developed white woman, and could only be compared with the brain of a white idiotic from arrest of cerebral development. Mr. Marshall has also recently examined the brain of a Bushwoman, and has discovered like evidence of structural inferiority : the primary convolutions, although all present, were smaller and much less complicated than in the European ; the external connecting convolutions were still more remarkably defective ; the secondary sulci and convolutions were everywhere decidedly less developed ;

there was a deficiency of transverse commissural fibres ;
and in size, and every one of the signs of comparative
inferiority, " it leaned, as it were, to the higher quadru-
manous forms." The developmental differences between
this brain and the brain of a European were in fact of
the same kind as, though less in degree than, those between the brain of an ape and that of man. Among
Europeans the average weight of the brain is greater in
educated than in uneducated persons ; its size—other circumstances being equal—bearing a general relation to the
mental power of the individual. Dr. Thurnam concludes,
from a series of carefully-compiled tables, that while
the average weight of the brain in ordinary Europeans
is 49 oz., it was 54'7 oz. in ten distinguished men ; and
Professor Wagner found a remarkably complex arrangement of the convolutions in the brains of five very eminent
men which he examined.[1] Thus, then, while we take it to

[1] The following table is compiled from Dr. Thurnam's paper " On
the Weight of the Human Brain " (*Journal of Mental Science,* April
1866) :—

BRAIN-WEIGHTS OF DISTINGUISHED MEN.

		Ages.	Oz.
1.	Cuvier, *Naturalist*	63	64'5
2.	Abercrombie, *Physician*	64	63
3.	Spurzheim, *Physician*	56	55'06
4.	Dirichlet, *Mathematician*	54	55'6
5.	De Morny, *Statesman and Courtier*	50	53'6
6.	Daniel Webster, *Statesman*	70	53'5
7.	Campbell, *Lord Chancellor*	80	53'5
8.	Chalmers, *celebrated Preacher*	67	53
9.	Fuchs, *Pathologist*	52	52'9
10.	Gauss, *Mathematician*	78	52'6
	Average of ten distinguished men	50–70	54'7

be well established that the convolutions of the human brain have undergone a considerable development through the ages, we may no less justly conclude that its larger, more numerous, and complex convolutions reproduce the higher and more varied mental activity to the progressive evolution of which their progressive increase has answered —that they manifest the kind of function which has determined the structure.   The vesicular neurine has increased in quantity and in quality, and the function of the increased and more highly-endowed structure is to display that intelligence which it unconsciously embodies. The native Australian, who is one of the lowest existing savages, has no words in his language to express such exalted ideas as justice, love, virtue, mercy; he has no such ideas in his mind, and cannot comprehend them. The vesicular neurine which should embody them in its constitution and manifest them in its function, has not been developed in his convolutions ; he is as incapable therefore of the higher mental displays of abstract reasoning and moral feeling as an idiot is, and for a like reason.   Indeed, were we to imagine a person born in this country, at this

		Ages.	Oz.
Brain-weights of average European men . .		20–60	49
		50–70	47·1
Average brain-weight of male negroes . . .			44·3
,, ,, 14 congenital idiots (males) .			42
,, ,, 8 ,, ,, (females) .			41·2
Estimated brain-weight of Microcephalic idiocy (males) .			37·5
,, ,, ,, (females)			32·5

It may be proper to add that the average weight of the adult male brain is 10 per cent. greater than that of the female—100 : 90.   The brains of the Hottentot, Bushman, and Australian are, so far as observation goes, of less weight than those of negroes.

time, with a brain of no higher development than the
brain of an Australian savage or a Bushman, it is perfectly
certain that he would be more or less of an imbecile.
And the only way, I suppose, in which beings of so low
an order of development could be raised to a civilized
level of feeling and thought would be by cultivation
continued through several generations; they would have
to undergo a gradual process of humanization before
they could attain to the capacity of civilization.

Some who one moment own freely the broad truth that
all mental manifestations take place through the brain go
on, nevertheless, to straightway deny that the conscience
or moral sensibility can be a function of organization.
But if all mental operations are not in this world equally
functions of organization, I know not what warrant we
have for declaring any to be so. The solution of the
much-vexed question concerning the origin of the moral
sense seems to lie in the considerations just adduced.
Are not, indeed, our moral intuitions results of the operation of the fundamental law of nervous organization by
which that which is consciously acquired becomes an
unconscious endowment, and is then transmitted as more
or less of an instinct to the next generation? They are
examples of knowledge which has been hardly gained
through the suffering and experience of the race,
being now inherited as a natural or instinctive sensibility
of the well-constituted brain of the individual. In the
matter of our moral feelings we are most truly the heirs
of the ages. Take the moral sense, and examine the
actions which it sanctions and those which it forbids, and

thus analyse, or, as it were, decompose, its nature, and it
will be found that the actions which it sanctions are those
which may be proved by sober reason to be conducive to
the well-being and the progress of the race, and that its
prohibitions fall upon the actions which, if freely indulged
in, would lead to the degeneration, if not extinction, of
mankind. And if we could imagine the human race to
live back again to its earliest infancy—to go backwards
through all the scenes and experiences through which it
has gone forward to its present height—and to give back
from its mind and character at each time and circum-
stance, as it passed it, exactly that which it gained when it
was there before,—should we not find the fragments and
exuviæ of the moral sense lying here and there along the
retrograde path, and a condition at the beginning which,
whether simian or human, was ·bare of all true moral
feeling ? [1]

We are daily witnesses of, and our daily actions testify
to, the operation of that plastic law of nervous organization by which separate and successive acquisitions are
combined and so intimately blended as to constitute
apparently a single and undecomposable faculty: we
observe it in the formation of our volitions; and we
observe it, in a more simple and less disputable form, in
the way in which combinations of movements that have
been slowly formed by practice are executed finally as

[1] Foster, in his "Essay on Decision of Character," makes this
conception of the individual character, almost in the words used ;
but the application of it to the race, and the conclusion drawn, are
of course not his.

easily as if they were a single and simple movement.   If
the moral sense—which is derived, then, insomuch as it
has been acquired in the process of human development
through the ages—were not more or less innate in the
well-born individual of this age, if he were obliged to go,
as the generations of his forefathers have gone, through
the elementary process of acquiring it, he would be very
much in the position of a person who, on each occasion
of writing his name, had to go through the elementary
steps of learning to do so.   The progressive evolution
of the human brain is a proof that we do inherit as a
natural endowment the laboured acquisitions of our
ancestors ; the added structure represents, as it were,
the embodied experience and memories of the race ; and
there is no greater difficulty in believing that the moral
sense may have been so formed, than in believing, what
has long been known and is admitted on all hands, that
the young fox or young dog inherits as an instinct the
special cunning which the foxes and the dogs that have
gone before it have had to win by hard experience.

These remarks are not an unnecessary digression.   Nor
will they have been made in vain if they serve to fix in
our minds the conviction that the law of progressive evolution and specialization of nerve-centres, which may be
traced generally from the first appearance of nerve tissue
in the lowest animals to the complex structure of the
nervous system of man, and specially from the rudimentary appearance of cerebral convolutions in the lower
vertebrata to the numerous and complex convolutions of
the human brain, does not abruptly cease its action at

the vesicular neurine of the hemispheres, but continues in force within the intimate recesses of the mental organization. Moreover, they are specially to the purpose, seeing that they enable us to understand in some sort how it is that a perversion or destruction of the moral sense is often one of the earliest symptoms of mental derangement : as the latest and most exquisite product of mental organization, the highest bloom of culture, it is the first to testify to disorder of the mind-centres. Not that we can detect any structural change in such case ; it is far too delicate for that. The wonder would, indeed, be if we could discover such more than microscopical changes with the instruments of research which we yet possess. We might almost as well look to discover the anatomy of a gnat with a telescope.

I purposely selected for consideration the defective brain of the idiot, because it exhibits an undeniable fault of structure, which is often plainly traceable to evil ancestral influences. When we duly consider this, and reflect that we might, if we chose, arrange a series of human brains which should present a regular gradation from the brain of an ape to that of a well-developed European, are we not fully justified in supposing that like unfavourable ancestral influences may occasion defects in the constitution or composition of the mind-centres which we are yet quite unable to detect ? We know nothing of the occult molecular movements which are the physical conditions of our mental operations ; we know little or nothing of the chemical changes which accompany them—cannot, in fact, detect the difference

between the nerve-element of a brain exhausted by exercise
and incapable of further function, and that of a brain
re-invigorated by sleep and ready for a day of energetic
function ; and we know nothing of the intricate connection
of nerve-cells in the hemispheres.   It is plain, then, that
there may be, unknown to us save as guessed from their
effects, the most important modifications in the molecular
activities of nerve-element, changes in its chemical composition, and actual defects in the physical constitution of
the nerve-centres.   Wherefore, when no appreciable defect
is found in the brain of one who has had a strong predisposition to insanity, and has ultimately died insane, it
behoves us to forbear a hasty conclusion that it is a perfectly well-constituted brain.   Close to us, yet inaccessible
to our senses, there lies a domain of nature—that of the
infinitely little,—the operations in which are as much
beyond our present ken as are those that take place in
the remotest regions of space, to which the eye, with all
its aids, cannot yet reach, and of which the mind cannot
conceive.

It certainly cannot be disputed that when nothing
abnormal whatever may be discoverable in the brains
of persons who have a strong hereditary tendency to
insanity, they often exhibit characteristic peculiarities in
their manner of thought, feeling, and conduct, carrying
in their physiognomy, bodily habit, and mental disposition
the sure marks of their evil heritage.   These marks are,
I believe, the outward and visible signs of an inward
and invisible peculiarity of cerebral organization.   Here,
indeed, we broach a most important inquiry, which has

only lately attracted attention—the inquiry, namely, into
the physical and mental signs of the degeneracy of the
human kind. I do not mean to assert that all persons
whose parents or blood relatives have suffered from
nervous or mental disease exhibit mental and bodily
peculiarities ; some may be well formed bodily and of
superior natural intelligence, the hereditary disposition in
them not having assumed the character of deterioration
of race ; but it admits of no dispute that there is what
may be called an *insane temperament* or *neurosis,* and that
it is marked by peculiarities of mental and bodily conformation.   Morel, who was the first to indicate, and has
done much to prosecute, this line of inquiry, looks upon
an individual so constituted as containing in himself the
germs of a morbid variety : summing up the pathological
elements which have been manifested by his ancestors,
he represents the first term of a series which, if nothing
happen to check the transmission of degenerate elements
from generation to generation, ends in the extreme degeneracy of idiocy, and in extinction of the family.

What are the bodily and mental marks of the insane
temperament ?   That there are such is most certain ; for
although the varieties of this temperament cannot yet be
described with any precision, no one who accustoms himself to observe closely will fail to be able to say positively,
in many instances, whether an insane person, and even a
sane person in some instances, comes of an insane family
or not.   An irregular and unsymmetrical conformation of
the head, a want of regularity and harmony of the
features, and, as Morel holds, malformations of the

external ear, are sometimes observed. Convulsions are apt to occur in early life; and there are tics, grimaces, or other spasmodic movements of muscles of face, eyelids, or lips afterwards. Stammering and defects of pronunciation are also sometimes signs of the neurosis. In other cases there are peculiarities of the eyes, which, though they may be full and prominent, have a vacillating movement, and a vacantly-abstracted, or half-fearful, half-suspicious, and distrustful look. There may, indeed, be something in the eye wonderfully suggestive of the look of an animal. The walk and manner are uncertain, and, though not easily described in words, may be distinctly peculiar. With these bodily traits are associated peculiarities of thought, feeling, and conduct. Without being insane, a person who has the insane neurosis strongly marked is thought to be strange, queer, and not like other persons. He is apt to see things under novel aspects, or to think about them under novel relations, which would not have occurred to an ordinary mortal. Punning on words is, I am inclined to think, sometimes an indication of the temperament, and so also that higher kind of wit which startles us with the use of an idea in a double sense; of both which aptitudes no better example can be given than that of Charles Lamb. His case, too, may show that the insane temperament is compatible with, and indeed it not seldom coexists with, considerable genius. Even those who have it in a more marked form often exhibit remarkable special talents and aptitudes, such as an extraordinary talent for music, or for calculation, or a prodigious memory for details, when they may be little better than imbecile in other things. There is, indeed, a marked instinctive character in all they think and do ; they seem not to need or to be able to reflect upon their own mental states. At one time unduly elated, at another time depressed without apparent cause, they are prone to do things differently from the rest of the world ; and now and then they do whimsical and seemingly quite purposeless acts, especially under conditions of excitement, when the impulses springing out of the unconscious morbid nature surprise and overpower them. Indeed, the mental balance may be easily upset altogether by any great moral shock, or by the strain of continued anxiety. A great physical change in the system, too, such as is caused by the development of puberty, by the puerperal state, and the climacteric change, is not without danger to their mental stability. The effects of alcohol on such persons are in some respects special : it does not make them so much drunk as mad for the time being ; and I think it will be found in most, if not all, cases of insanity caused by alcohol that there has been a predisposition to it.

I have sketched generally the features of the insane temperament, but there are really several varieties of it which need to be observed and described. In practice we meet with individuals representing every gradation from the mildest form of the insane temperament down to actual idiocy. These cases ought to be arranged in groups according to their affinities, for until this be done we shall not make much real progress towards exact scientific notions respecting the causation and pathology of insanity.   One group might consist of those egotistic beings, having the insane neurosis, who manifest a peculiar morbid suspicion of everything and everybody; they detect an interested or malicious motive in the most innocent actions of others, always looking out for an evil interpretation; and even events they regard as in a sort of conspiracy against them.   Incapable of altruistic reflection and true sympathies, they live a life of solitude and self-brooding, entrenched within their morbid self-feeling, until the discord between them and the world is so great that there is nothing for it but to count them mad. Another group might be made of those persons of unsound mental temperament who are born with an entire absence of the moral sense, destitute of the possibility even of moral feeling; they are as truly insensible to the moral relations of life, as deficient in this regard, as a person colour-blind is to certain colours, or as one who is without ear for music is to the finest harmonies of sound. Although there is usually conjoined with this absence of moral sensibility more or less weakness of mind, it does happen in some instances that there is a remarkably acute intellect of the cunning type.

The observations of intelligent prison surgeons are tending more and more to prove that a considerable proportion of criminals are weak-minded or epileptic, or come of families in which insanity, epilepsy, or some other neurosis exists.   Mr. Thompson, surgeon to the General Prison of Scotland, has gone so far recently as to express his conviction that the principal business of prison surgeons must always be with mental defects or disease;

F

that the diseases and causes of death among prisoners are chiefly of the nervous system ; and, in fine, that the treatment of crime is a branch of psychology. He holds that there is among criminals a distinct and incurable *criminal class*, marked by peculiar low physical and mental characteristics ; that crime is hereditary in the families of criminals belonging to this class ; and that this hereditary crime is a disorder of mind, having close relations of nature and descent to epilepsy, dipsomania, insanity, and other forms of degeneracy. Such criminals are really *morbid varieties*, and often exhibit marks of physical degeneration—spinal deformities, stammering, imperfect organs of speech, club-foot, cleft palate, hare-lip, deafness, paralysis, epilepsy, and scrofula. Moreau relates a striking case, which is of interest as indicating the alliance between morbid or degenerate varieties, and which I may quote here.

Mrs. D——, aged thirty-two. Her grandfather kept an inn at the time of the great French Revolution, and during the Reign of Terror he had profited by the critical situation in which many nobles of the department found themselves to get them secretly into his house, where he was believed to have robbed and murdered them. His daughter, who was in his secrets, having quarrelled with him, denounced him to the authorities, but he escaped conviction from want of proofs. She subsequently committed suicide. One of her brothers had nearly murdered her with a knife on one occasion, and another brother hanged himself. Her sister was epileptic, imbecile, and paroxysmally violent. Her daughter, the patient, after swimming in the head, noises in the ears, flashes before the eyes, became deranged, fancying that people were plotting against her, purchasing arms and barricading herself in her room, and was finally put in an asylum. Thus there were, in different members of this family, crime, melancholia, epilepsy, suicide, and mania. Need we wonder at it ? The moral element is an essential part of a complete and sound character ; he who is destitute of it, being unquestionably to that extent a defective being, is therefore on the road to, or marks, race degeneracy ; and it is not a matter of much wonder that his children should, when better influences do not intervene to check the morbid tendency, exhibit a further degree of degeneracy, and be actual morbid varieties. I think that no one who has studied closely the causation of insanity will question this mode of production.

I could not, if I would, in the present state of know-ledge, describe accurately all the characteristics of the insane neurosis, and group according to their affinities the cases testifying to its influence. The chief concern now with its morbid peculiarities is to point out, first, that they mark some inherited fault of brain-organization ; and, secondly, that the cause of such fault is not insanity alone in the parent, but may be other nervous disease, such as hysteria, epilepsy, alcoholism, paralysis, and neuralgia of all kinds. Except in the case of suicidal insanity, it is not usual for the parent to transmit to the child the particular form of mental derangement from which he has suffered : insanity in the parent may be epilepsy in the child, and epilepsy in the parent insanity

in the child; and in families where a strong tendency
to insanity exists, one member may be insane, another
epileptic, a third may suffer from severe neuralgia, and a
fourth may commit suicide.   The morbid conditions
which affect the motor nerve-centres in one generation
seem to concentrate themselves sometimes upon the
sensory or the ideational centres in another.   In truth,
nervous disease is a veritable Proteus, disappearing in
one form to reappear in another, and, it may be, capriciously skipping one generation to fasten upon the next.

The different forms of insanity that occur in young
children—as all forms of it except general paralysis may
do—are almost always traceable to nervous disease in
the preceding generation, a neuropathic condition being
really the essential element in their causation.   The
cases of acute mania in children of a few weeks or a few
years old which have been described might more properly be classed as examples of idiocy with excitement.
There can be no true mania until there is some mind.
But we do meet sometimes in older children with a
genuine acute mania, occurring usually in connection with
chorea or epilepsy, and presenting the symptoms, if I
may so express it, of a mental chorea or an epilepsy of
the mind, but without the spasmodic and convulsive
movements of these diseases.   More or less dulness of
intelligence and apathy of movement, giving the seeming
of a degree of imbecility, is common enough in chorea, and
in some cases there is violent delirium; but, besides these
cases, there are others in which, without choreic disorder
of movements, there is a choreic mania : it is an active

delirium of ideas which is the counterpart of the usual
delirium of movements, and its automatic character and
its marked incoherence are striking enough to an ordinary
observer. Hallucinations of the special senses, and loss
or perversion of general sensibility, usually accompany
the delirium, the disorder affecting the centres of special
and general sensation, as well as the mind-centres.

Between this choreic mania and epileptic mania there
are intermediate conditions partaking more or less of the
character of one or the other—hybrid forms of a cataleptic nature. The child will lie for hours or days in a
seeming ecstasy or trance, with its limbs rigid or fixed
in a strange posture. There may be apparent insen-
sibility to impressions, while at other times vague
answers are given, or there is a sudden bursting out into
wild shrieks or incoherent raving. If this be of a religious kind, the child is apt to be thought by ignorant persons to be inspired. The attacks are of variable duration,
and are repeated at varying intervals. On the one hand
they pass into attacks of chorea ; and, on the other hand,
into true epileptic seizures, or alternate with them.

In children, as in adults, a brief attack of violent
mania, a genuine *mania transitoria,* may precede, or follow, or take the place of an epileptic fit ; in the latter
case being a masked epilepsy. Children of three or
four years of age are sometimes seized with attacks of
violent shrieking, desperate stubbornness, or furious rage,
when they bite, tear, kick, and do all the destruction they
can ; these seizures, which are a sort of vicarious epilepsy,
come on periodically, and may either pass in the course

of a few months into regular epilepsy, or may alternate
with it.   Older children have perpetrated crimes of a
savage and determined nature—incendiarism and even
murder—under the influence of similar attacks of transitory fury, followed or not by epileptic convulsions.
It is of the utmost importance to realize the deep effect
which the epileptic neurosis may have on the moral
character, and to keep in mind the possibility of its existence when a savage, apparently motiveless, and unaccountable crime has been committed.   A single epileptic seizure has been known to change entirely the moral
character, rendering a child rude, vicious, and perverse,
who was hitherto gentle, amiable, and tractable.   No one
who has seen it can fail to have been struck with the
great and abrupt change in moral character which
takes place in the asylum epileptic immediately before
the recurrence of his fits; in the intervals between them
he is often an amiable, obliging, and industrious being, but
when they impend he becomes sullen, morose, and most
dangerous to meddle with.   Not an attendant but can
then foretell that he is going to have his fits, as confidently almost as he can foretell that the sun will rise next
day.   Morel has made the interesting observation, which
is certainly well founded, that the epileptic neurosis may
exist for a considerable period in an undeveloped or
masked form, showing itself, not by convulsions, but by
periodic attacks of mania, or by manifestations of extreme moral perversion, which are apt to be thought
wilful viciousness.   But they are not: no moral influence
will touch them ; they depend upon a morbid physical

condition, which can only have a physical cure; and
they get their explanation, and indeed justification, afterwards, when actual epilepsy occurs.

The epileptic neurosis is certainly most closely allied
to the insane neurosis; and when it exists in its masked
form, affecting the mind for some time before convulsions
occur, it is hardly possible to distinguish it from one
form of the insane neurosis. The difficulty of doing so
is made greater, inasmuch as epilepsy in the parent may
engender the insane neurosis in the child, and insanity
in the parent the epileptic neurosis in the child. A
character which the insane neurosis has in common with
the epileptic neurosis is, that it is apt to burst out in a
convulsive explosion of violence; that when it develops
into actual insanity it displays itself in deeds rather than
in words—in an insanity of action rather than of thought.
It is truly a *neurosis spasmodica.* Take, for example, a
case which is one of a class, that of the late Alton mur-
derer, who, taking a walk one fine afternoon, met some
little girls at play, enticed one of them into a neigh-
bouring hop-garden, there murdered her and cut her
body into fragments, which he scattered about, returned
quietly home, openly washing his hands in the river on
the way, made an entry in his diary, "Killed a little
girl; it was fine and hot;" and when forthwith taken into
custody, confessed what he had done, and could give no
reason for doing it. At the trial it was proved that his
father had had an attack of acute mania, and that another
near relative was in confinement, suffering from homicidal
mania. He himself had been noted as peculiar; he had

been subject to fits of depression, been prone to weep without apparent reason, and had exhibited singular caprices of conduct; and it had once been necessary to watch him from fear that he might commit suicide. He was not insane in the legal or the ordinary sense of the term, but he certainly had the insane neurosis, and it may be presumed confidently that he would, had he lived, have become insane.

Those who have practical experience of insanity know well that there is a most distressing form of the disease, in which a desperate impulse to commit suicide or homicide overpowers and takes prisoner the reason. The terrible impulse is deplored sometimes by him who suffers from it as deeply as by anyone who witnesses it; it causes him unspeakable distress; he is fully conscious of its nature, and struggles in vain against it; his reason is no further affected than in having lost power to control, or having become the slave of, the morbid and convulsive impulse. It may be that this form of derangement does sometimes occur where there is no hereditary predisposition to insanity, but there can be no doubt that in the great majority of cases of the kind there is such a neuropathic state. The impulse is truly a convulsive idea, springing from a morbid condition of nerve element, and it is strictly comparable with an epileptic convulsion. How grossly unjust, then, the judicial criterion of responsibility which dooms an insane person of this class to death if he knew what he was doing when he committed a murder! It were as reasonable to hang a man for not stopping by an act of will a convul-

sion of which he was conscious. An interesting circum-
stance in connection with this morbid impulse is that its
convulsive activity is sometimes preceded by a feeling
very like the *aura epileptica*—a strange morbid sensation,
beginning in some part of the body, and rising gradually
to the brain. The patient may accordingly give warning
of the impending attack in some instances, and in one
case was calmed by having his thumbs loosely tied
together with a ribbon when the forewarning occurred.
Dr. Skae records an instructive example in one of his
annual reports. The feeling began at the toes, rose
gradually to the chest, producing a sense of faintness
and constriction, and then to the head, producing a
momentary loss of consciousness. This aura was accompanied by an involuntary jerking—first of the legs, and
then of the arms. It was when these attacks came on
that the patient felt impelled to commit some act of
violence against others or himself. On one occasion he
attempted to commit suicide by throwing himself into
the water ; more often the impulse was to attack others.
He deplored his condition, of which he spoke with great
intelligence, giving all the details of his past history and
feelings. In other cases a feeling of vertigo, a trembling,
and a vague dread of something fearful being about to
happen, resembling the vertigo and momentary vague
despair of one variety of the epileptic aura, precede the
attack. Indeed, whenever a murder has been committed
suddenly, without premeditation, without malice, without
motive, openly, and in a way quite different from the
way in which murders are commonly done, we ought to

look carefully for evidence of previous epilepsy, and, should there have been no epileptic fits, for evidence of an *aura epileptica* and other symptoms allied to epilepsy.

It is worth while observing that in other forms of insanity, when we look closely into the symptoms, there are not unfrequently complaints of strange, painful, and distressing sensations in some part of the body, which appear to have a relation to the mental derangement not unlike that which the epileptic aura has to the epileptic fit. Common enough is a distressing sensation about the epigastrium : it is not a definite pain, is not comparable strictly to a burning, or weight, or to any known sensation, but is an indescribable feeling of distress to which the mental troubles are referred. It sometimes rises to a pitch of anguish, when it abolishes the power to think, destroys the feeling of identity, and causes such unspeakable suffering and despair that suicide is attempted or accomplished. In other cases the distressing and indescribable sensation is in the crown of the head or down the spine, and sometimes it arises from the pelvic organs. In all cases the patients connect their mental trouble with it, regarding it as the cause of the painful confusion of thought, the utter inability of exertion, the distressing ideas, and the paroxysm of despair. Perhaps they exaggerate its importance ; but there can be little doubt that writers on mental disorders, too exclusively occupied with the prominent mental features, have not hitherto given sufficient attention to these anomalous sensations. We have been apt to class them as hypochondriacal, and to pass them over

as of no special significance ; but I cannot help thinking that, properly studied, they may sometimes teach
us more of the real nature of the particular form of insanity—of its probable course, termination, and its most
suitable treatment—than many much more obtrusive
symptoms.

In bringing this lecture to an end, I may fitly point
out how entirely thus far the observation of the phenomena of defective and disordered mind proves their
essential dependence on defective and disordered brain,
and how closely they are related to some other disordered
nervous functions. The insane neurosis which the child
inherits in consequence of its parent's insanity is as
surely a defect of physical nature as is the epileptic
neurosis to which it is so closely allied. It is an indis-
putable though extreme fact that certain human beings
are born with such a native deficiency of mind that all
the training and education in the world will not raise
them to the height of brutes ; and I believe it to be not
less true that, in consequence of evil ancestral influences,
individuals are born with such a flaw or warp of nature
that all the care in the world will not prevent them from
being vicious or criminal, or becoming insane. Education, it is true, may do much, and the circumstances of
life may do much ; but we cannot forget that the foundations on which the acquisitions of education must rest
are not acquired, but inherited. No one can escape the
tyranny of his organization ; no one can elude the destiny
that is innate in him, and which unconsciously and
irresistibly shapes his ends, even when he believes that

76 *BODY AND MIND.* [LECT. II.

he is determining them with consummate foresight and
skill.   A well-grounded and comprehensive theory of
mind must recognize and embrace these facts ; they
meet us every moment of our lives, and cannot be ignored
if we are in earnest in our attempts to construct a mental
science ; and it is because metaphysical mental philosophy has taken no notice whatever of them, because it
is bound by the principle of its existence as a philosophy
to ignore them, that, notwithstanding the labour bestowed
on it, it has borne no fruits—that, as Bacon said of
it, "not only what was asserted once is asserted still,
but what were questions once are questions still, and,
instead of being resolved by discussion, are only fixed
and fed."

LECTURE III.

GENTLEMEN,—In my last lecture I showed how large a part in the production of insanity is played by the hereditary neurosis, and pointed out the necessity of scrutinizing more closely than has yet been done the features of the different forms of mental derangement that own its baneful influence. Past all question it is the most important element in the causation of insanity. It cannot be in the normal order of events that a healthy organism should be unable to bear ordinary mental trials, much less a natural physiological function such as the evolution of puberty, the puerperal state, or the climacteric change. When, therefore, the strain of grief or one of these physiological conditions becomes the occasion of an outbreak of insanity, we must look for the root of the ill in some natural infirmity or instability of nerve element. Not until we apply ourselves earnestly to an exact observation and discrimination of all the mental and bodily conditions which co-operate in the causation, and are manifested in the symptoms, of the manifold varieties of insanity, shall

we render more precise and satisfactory our knowledge
of its causes, its classification, and its treatment. How
unscientific it appears, when we reflect, to enumerate, as
is commonly done, sex and age amongst its predisposing
causes ! No one goes mad because he or she happens
to be a man or a woman, but because to each sex,
and at certain ages, there occur special physiological
changes, which are apt to run into pathological effects
in persons predisposed to nervous disorder. How often
it happens that a moral cause of insanity is sought
and falsely found in a state of mind such as grief or
jealousy, which is really an early symptom of the
disease ! Again, how vague and . unsatisfactory the
accepted psychological classification of insanity, under
which forms of disease distinct enough to claim separate
descriptions are included in the same class ! It is
obvious that . we learn very little of value from an
account of the treatment of mania generally when
there are included under the class diseases so different
as puerperal mania, the mania of general paralysis,
syphilitic, epileptic, and hysterical mania, each presenting
features and requiring treatment in some degree special.
The hope and the way of advance in our knowledge
of mental disorders lie in the exact observation of the
varieties of the insane diathesis, and of the effects of
bodily functions and disorders upon these ; in noting
carefully the bodily as well as mental symptoms that
characterize the several forms of derangement of mind ;
and in tracing the relations of mental to other disorders
of the nervous system. We must aim to distinguish

well if we would teach well—to separate the cases that
exhibit special features and relations, and to arrange
them in groups or classes according to their affinities,
just as we do habitually with general paralysis, and as
I did in my last lecture with epileptic mania.

Following this plan, we might in like manner make
of *hysterical* insanity a special variety. - An attack of
acute maniacal excitement, with great restlessness, rapid
and disconnected but not entirely incoherent conver-
sation, sometimes tending to the erotic or obscene,
evidently without abolition of consciousness; laughing,
singing, or rhyming, and perverseness of conduct, which
is still more or less coherent and seemingly wilful,
—may occur in connection with, or instead of, the
usual hysterical convulsions. Or the ordinary hysterical
symptoms may pass by degrees into chronic insanity.
Loss of power of will is a characteristic symptom of
hysteria in all its Protean forms, and with the perverted
sensations and disordered movements there is always
some degree of moral perversion. This increases until
it swallows up the other symptoms : the patient loses
more and more of her energy and self-control, becoming
capriciously fanciful about her health, imagining or
feigning strange diseases, and keeping up the delusion
or the imposture with a pertinacity that might seem
incredible, getting more and more impatient of the
advice and interference of others, and indifferent to
the interests and duties of her position. Outbursts of
temper become almost outbreaks of mania, particularly
at the menstrual periods. An erotic tinge may be

observable in her manner of behaviour; and occasionally
there are quasi-ecstatic or cataleptic states. It is an
easily curable form of derangement if the patient be
removed in time from the anxious but hurtful sympathies
and attentions of her family, and placed under good
moral control; but if it be allowed to go on unchecked,
it will end in dementia, and it is especially apt to do
so when there is a marked hereditary predisposition.

In some instances we observe a curious connection
between insanity and neuralgia, not unlike that which,
existing between epilepsy and a special form of neuralgia,
induced Trousseau to describe the latter as epileptiform.
I have under observation now a lady who suffered
for some time from an intense neuralgia of the left half
of the face; after the removal of a tooth suspected
to be at the root of the mischief the pain ceased, but an
attack of melancholia immediately followed. Griesinger
mentions a similar case of a gentleman under his care,
in whom a double occipital neuralgia was followed by
a melancholic state of mind. In his " Commentaries
on Insanity " Dr. Burrows tells of a very eloquent divine
who was always maniacal when free from pains in the
spine, and sane when the pains returned to that site.
And the late Sir B. Brodie mentions two cases of a
similar kind: in one of them a neuralgia of the
vertebral column alternated with true insanity. These
cases appear to be instances of the transference of
morbid action from one nerve-centre to another such
as Dr. Darwin formerly noticed and commented on.
"Mrs. C——," he says, "was seized every day, about

the same hour, with violent pain in the right side of her bowels, about the situation of the lower edge of the liver, without fever, which increased for an hour or two, till it became quite intolerable. After violent screaming she fell into convulsions, which terminated sometimes in fainting, with or without stertor, as in common epilepsy; at other times a temporary insanity supervened, which continued about half an hour, and the fit ceased." It seems not unreasonable to suppose that the morbid action in the sensory centres, which the violent neuralgia implied, was at one time transferred to the motor centres, giving rise to convulsive movements, and at another time to the mind-centres, giving rise to convulsive ideas. There is a form of neuralgia which is the analogue of a convulsion, and there is a mania which is the counterpart, in the highest nerve-centres, of neuralgia and convulsions in their respective centres. Perhaps if we had the power in some cases of acute insanity to induce artificially a violent neuralgia, or general convulsions—to transfer the morbid action from the mind-centres—we might, for the time being at any rate, cure the insanity.

I pass on now to exhibit the effects of organic sympathies in the causation of mental disorders, or rather the specific effects of particular organs upon the features of different forms of insanity. In my first lecture I pointed out that there is the closest physiological consent of functions between the different organs; that the brain, as the organ of mind, joins in this consent; and tha our ideas and feelings are obtained by the concurrence of impressions from the internal organs of the body and the external organs of the senses. The consequence is that derangement of an internal organ, acting upon the brain, may engender, by pathological sympathy, morbid feelings and their related ideas. The mental effects may be general or specific : a general emotional depression through which all ideas loom gloomy, of which every one's experience testifies ; and a special morbid feeling with its particular sympathetic ideas, of which the phenomena of dreaming and insanity yield illustrations.

The slight shades of this kind of morbid influence we cannot venture to trace ; but it is easy to recognize the most marked effects. Take, for example, the irritation of ovaries or uterus, which is sometimes the direct occasion of *nymphomania*—a disease by which the most chaste and modest woman is transformed into a raging fury of lust. Some observers have, without sufficient reason I think, made of *nymphomania* a special variety, grouping under the term cases in which it was a prominent symptom. But it certainly occurs in forms of mania that are quite distinct—in puerperal mania, for example, in epileptic mania, and in the mania sometimes met with in old women ; and the cases in which it does occur have not such characteristic features as warrant the formation of a definite group. We have, indeed, to note and bear in mind how often sexual ideas and feelings arise and display themselves in all sorts of insanity ; how they connect themselves with ideas which in a normal mental state have no known relation to them ; so that it seems as inexplicable that a virtuous person should ever have learnt, as it is distressing that she should manifest, so much obscenity of thought and feeling. Perhaps it is that such ideas are excited sympathetically in a morbidly active brain by unrelated ideas, just as, in other nervous disorders, sympathetic morbid sensations and movements occur in parts distant from the seat of the primary irritation. Considering, too, what an important agent in the evolution of mind the sexual feeling is, how much of thought, feeling, and energy it remotely inspires, there is less cause for wonder at the naked intervention of its simple impulses in the phenomena of mania, when co-ordination of function is abolished in the supreme centres, and the mind resolved, as it were, into its primitive animal elements. This should teach us to take care not to attribute too hastily the sexual feelings to a morbid irritation of the sexual organs. It is plain that they may have a purely central origin, just as the excitation of them in health may proceed from the mind. Here, in fact, as in other cases, we must bear in mind the reciprocal influence of mind on organ, and of organ on mind.

The great mental revolution which occurs at puberty may go beyond its physiological limits, in some instances, and become pathological. The vague feelings, blind longings, and obscure impulses which then arise in the mind attest the awakening of an impulse which knows not at first its aim or the means of its gratification ; a kind of vague and yearning melancholy is engendered, which leads to an abandonment to poetry of a gloomy

Byronic kind, or to indulgence in indefinite religious
feelings and aspirations. There is a want of some
object to fill the void in the feelings, to satisfy the
undefined yearning—a need of something to adore;
consequently, where there is no visible object of worship
the invisible is adored. The time of this mental revolution is, at best, a trying period for youth; and where
there is an inherited infirmity of nervous organization,
the natural disturbance of the mental balance may easily
pass into actual destruction of it.

The form of derangement connected with this period
of life I believe to be either a fanciful and quasi-
hysterical melancholia, which is not very serious when
it is properly treated; or an acute mania, which is apt
to be recurrent, and is much more serious. The former
occurs especially in girls, if it be not peculiar to them :
there are periods of depression and paroxysms of
apparently causeless weeping, alternating with times
of undue excitability, more especially at the menstrual
periods; a disinclination is evinced to work, to rational
amusement, to exertion of any kind; the behaviour is
capricious, and soon becomes perverse and wilful; the
natural affections seem to be blunted or abolished, the
patient taking pleasure in distressing those whose feelings
she would most consider when in health ; and, although
there are no fixed delusions, there are unfounded
suspicions or fears and changing morbid fancies. The
anxious sympathies of those most dear are apt to foster
the morbid self-feeling which craves them, and thus to
aggravate the disease: what such patients need to learn

is, not the indulgence but a forgetfulness of their feelings,, not the observation but the renunciation of self, not introspection but useful action.   In some of these cases, where the disease has become chronic, delusions of sexual origin occur, and the patient whose virginity is intact imagines that she is pregnant or has had a baby.

The morbid self-feeling that has its root in the sexual system is not unapt to take on a religious guise. We observe examples of this in certain members of those latter-day religious sects which profess to commingle religion and love, and which especially abound in America. No physiologist can well doubt that the holy kiss of love in such cases owes all its warmth to the sexual feeling which consciously or unconsciously inspires it, or that the mystical union of the sexes lies very close to a union that is nowise mystical, when it does not lead to madness. A similar intimate connection between fanatical religious exaltation and sexual excitement is exemplified by the lives of such religious enthusiasts as St. Theresa and St. Catherine de Sienne, whose nightly trances and visions, in which they believed themselves received as veritable spouses into the bosom of Christ and transported into an unspeakable ecstasy by the touch of His sacred lips, attested, though they knew it not, the influence of excited sexual organs on the mind.   More extreme examples of a like pathological action are afforded by those insane women who believe themselves to be visited by lovers or ravished by persecutors during the night. Sexual hallucinations, betraying an ovarian or uterine excitement, might almost be described as the characteristic feature of the insanity of old maids ; the false visions of unreal indulgence being engendered probably in the same way as visions of banquets occur in the dreams of a starving person, or as visions of cooling streams to one who is perishing of thirst. It seems to be the fact that, although women bear sexual excesses better than men, they suffer more than men do from the entire deprivation of sexual intercourse.

The development of puberty may lead indirectly to nsanity by becoming the occasion of a vicious habit of self-abuse in men ; and it is not always easy to say in such cases how much of the evil is due to pubescence and how much to self-abuse. But the form of mental derangement directly traceable to self-abuse has certainly characteristic features. There are no acute symptoms, the onset of the disease being most gradual. The patient becomes offensively egotistic and impracticable ; he is full of self-feeling and self-conceit ; insensible to the claims of others upon him, and of his duties to them ; interested only in hypochondriacally watching his morbid sensations, and attending to his morbid feelings. His mental energy is sapped ; and though he has extravagant pretensions, and often speaks of great projects engendered by his conceit, he never works systematically for any aim, but exhibits an incredible vacillation of conduct, and spends his days in indolent and suspicious self-brooding. His relatives he thinks hostile to him, because they do not take the interest in his sufferings which he craves, nor yield sufficiently to his pretensions, but perhaps urge him to some kind of work ; he is utterly incapable of conceiving that he has duties to them. As matters get worse, the general suspicion of the hostility of people takes more definite form, and delusions spring up that persons speak offensively of him, or watch him in the street, or comment on what passes in his mind, or play tricks upon him by electricity or mesmerism, or in some other mysterious way. His delusions are the objective explanation, by wrong imagination, of the perverted feelings. Messages may be received from heaven by peculiar telegraphic signals; and there are occasionally quasi-cataleptic trances. It is strange what exalted feelings and high moral and religious aims these patients will often declare they have, who, incapable of reforming themselves, are ready to reform the world. A later and worse stage is one of moody or vacant self-absorption, and of extreme loss of mental power. They are silent, or, if they converse, they discover delusions of a suspicious or obscene character, the perverted sexual passion still giving the colour to their thoughts. They die miserable wrecks at the last. This is a form of insanity which certainly has its special exciting cause and its characteristic features ; nevertheless, I think that self-abuse seldom, if ever, produces it without the co-operation of the insane neurosis.

The monthly activity of the ovaries which marks the advent of puberty in women has a notable effect upon the mind and body; wherefore it may become an important cause of mental and physical derangement. Most women at that time are susceptible, irritable, and capricious, any cause of vexation affecting them more

seriously than usual; and some who have the insane
neurosis exhibit a disturbance of mind which amounts
almost to disease. A sudden suppression of the menses
has produced a direct explosion of insanity; or, occurring some time before an outbreak, it may be an important link in its causation. It is a matter also of common
experience in asylums, that exacerbations of insanity
often take place at the menstrual periods; but whether
there is a particular variety of mental derangement connected with disordered menstruation, and, if so, what are
its special features, we are not yet in a position to say
positively. There is certainly a recurrent mania, which
seems sometimes to have, in regard to its origin and the
times of its attacks, a relation to the menstrual function,
suppression or irregularity of which often accompanies
it; and it is an obvious presumption that the mania may
be a sympathetic morbid effect of the ovarian and uterine
excitement, and may represent an exaggeration of the
mental irritability which is natural to women at that
period. The patient becomes elated, hilarious, talkative,
passing soon from that condition into a state of acute
and noisy mania, which may last for two or three weeks
or longer, and then sinking into a brief stage of more or
less depression or confusion of mind, from which she
awakens to calmness and clearness of mind. In vain
we flatter ourselves with the hope of a complete recovery; after an interval of perfect lucidity, of varying
duration in different cases, the attack recurs, goes through
the same stages, and ends in the same way, only to be
followed by other attacks, until at last, the mind being

permanently weakened, there are no longer intervals of
entire lucidity.   Could we stop the attacks, the patient
might still regain by degrees mental power; but we
cannot.   All the resources of our art fail to touch them,
and I know no other form of insanity which, having so
much the air of being curable, thus far defies all efforts
to stay its course.   We should be apt to conclude that
it was connected with the menstrual function, were it not
that periodicity is more or less the law of all nervous
diseases, that its attacks often recur at uncertain intervals,
and, more decisive still, that it is not confined to women,
but occurs perhaps as often in men.   Whether connected
or not, however, in any way with the generative functions,
it certainly presents features of relationship to epilepsy,
and occurs where the insane neurosis exists; and if I
were to describe it in a few words, I should designate it
an epilepsy of the mind.   Its recurrence more or less
regularly; the uniformity of the prodromata and of the
symptoms of the attack, each being almost an exact
image of the other; its comparatively brief duration ;
the mental torpor or confusion which follows it, and the
ignorance or denial sometimes on the part of the patient,
of his having had the attack ; the temporary recovery ;
and the undoubted fact that it often occurs where there
is evidence of an insane neurosis produced by epilepsy,
or insanity, or both, in the family ;—these are facts which
support the opinion of its kinship to epilepsy.   I have
under my care an unmarried lady who for many years
has been subject to these recurrent attacks of mania, and
whose intelligence has now been destroyed by them ;

ultimately true epileptic fits supervened, but they only
occur, at long intervals, usually not oftener than twice
a year, while the maniacal attacks recur regularly every
three or four weeks.   It is of some interest, in regard
to the question of its nature, that the age of its most
frequent outbreak is, as it is with epilepsy, the years that
cover the development of puberty.   Irregularity or suppression of menstruation may or may not be present, so
that we are not warranted in attributing the disease to
amenorrhœa or dysmenorrhœa ; we are the less warranted
in doing so, as any form of insanity, however caused, may
occasion a suppression of the menses.

The natural cessation of menstruation at the change of
life is accompanied by a revolution in the economy which
is often trying to the mental stability of those who have
a predisposition to insanity.   The age of pleasing is past,
but not always the desire, which, indeed, sometimes
grows then more exacting ; there are all sorts of anomalous
sensations of bodily distress, attesting the disturbance of
circulation and of nerve functions ; and it is now that an
insane jealousy and a propensity to stimulants are apt
to appear, especially where there have been no children.
When positive insanity breaks out, it usually has the form
of profound melancholia, with vague delusions of an
extreme character, as that the world is in flames, that
it is turned upside down, that everything is changed,
or that some very dreadful but undefined calamity has
happened or is about to happen.   The countenance has
the expression of a vague terror and apprehension.   In
some cases short and transient paroxysms of excitement

break the melancholy gloom. These usually occur at the menstrual periods, and may continue to do so for some time after the function has ceased. It is not an unfavourable form of insanity as regards probability of recovery under suitable treatment.

Continuing the consideration of the influence of the generative organs in the production of insanity, I come now to puerperal insanity. Under this name are sometimes confounded three distinct varieties of disease—that which occurs during pregnancy, that which follows parturition and is properly puerperal, and that which comes on months afterwards during lactation.[1] The insanity of pregnancy is, as a rule, of a marked melancholic type, with suicidal tendency; a degree of mental weakness or apparent dementia being sometimes conjoined with it. Other cases, however, exhibit much moral perversion, perhaps an uncontrollable craving for stimulants, which we may regard as an exaggerated display of the fanciful cravings from which women suffer in the earlier months of pregnancy. We can hardly fail, indeed, to recognize a connection between the features of this form of insanity and the strange longings, the capriciousness, and the morbid fears of the pregnant woman. The patient may be treated successfully by removal from home; but if the disease be allowed to go on, there is no good ground to expect that parturition will have a beneficial effect upon it; on the contrary, the probability is that it will run into a severe puerperal insanity, and from that into dementia.

[1] "The Insanity of Pregnancy, Puerperal Insanity, and Insanity of Lactation." By J. Batty Tuke, M.D.

Puerperal insanity proper comes on within one month of parturition; and, like the insanity of pregnancy, occurs most often in primiparæ. The statistics of the Edinburgh Asylum show that in all the cases occurring before the sixteenth day after labour, as most cases do, the symptoms were those of acute mania; but in all the cases which occurred after the sixteenth day they were those of melancholia. In both forms, but especially in the latter, there is sometimes a mixture of childishness and apparent dementia. The mania is more likely than the melancholia to get well. It is of an acute and extremely incoherent character, a delirious rather than a systematized mania, marked by noisy restlessness, sleeplessness, tearing of clothes, hallucinations, and in some cases by great salacity, which is probably the direct mental effect of the irritation of the generative organs. Suicide may be attempted in an excited, purposeless way. The bodily symptoms, contradicting the violence of the mental excitement, indicate feebleness : the features are pinched; the skin is pale, cold, and clammy; and the pulse is quick, small, and irritable. We may safely say that recovery takes place in three out of four cases of puerperal mania, usually in a few weeks; the patient, after the acute symptoms have subsided, sinking into a temporary state of confusion and feebleness of mind, and then waking up as from a dream. I may add the expression of a conviction that no good, but rather harm, is done by attempting to stifle this or any other form of acute insanity by the administration of large doses of opium.

The insanity of lactation does not come under the

scheme of this lecture; for it is an asthenic insanity, produced by bodily exhaustion and the depression of mental worries. The time of its occurrence seems to show that the longer the child is suckled the greater is the liability to it; and in the majority of cases it has the form of melancholia, often with determined suicidal tendency.

So frequently is hereditary predisposition more or less distinctly traceable in these three forms of insanity occurring in connection with child-bearing, that we are warranted in declaring it quite exceptional for any one of them to be met with where it is entirely absent.

I have now enumerated all the forms of insanity which, being specially connected with the generative organs, present characteristic features. It is certain, however, that disease of them may act as a powerful co-operating cause in the production of insanity, without giving rise, so far as we know, to a special group of symptoms. Thus, for example, melancholia, distinguishable by no feature from melancholia otherwise caused, may be the effect of disease of the uterus. Schröder van der Kolk mentions the case of a woman profoundly melancholic who suffered from prolapsus uteri, and in whom the melancholia disappeared when the uterus was returned to its proper place. Flemming relates two similar cases in which melancholia was cured by the use of a pessary, the depression returning in one of them whenever the pessary was removed; and I have met with one case in which profound melancholia of two years' standing disappeared after the removal of a prolapsus uteri. Other diseases

and displacements of the uterus may act in a similar
way.

Let me now say a few words concerning the abdominal organs. No one will call in question that the states
of their functions do exert a positive influence on our
states of mind; but it is unfortunately too true that we
cannot yet refer any special mental symptoms to the influence of the abdominal organs. I have met with one
case of severe melancholia, of long standing, which was
distinctly cured by the expulsion of a tapeworm; and it
appears to be tolerably certain that hypochondriacal insanity is in some instances connected with, if not caused
by, a perverted sensation proceeding from an internal
organ, most often abdominal. In health we are not conscious of the impressions which these organs make upon
the brain, albeit they assuredly send their unperceived
contributions to the stream of energies of which consciousness is the sum and the outcome; but when a disordered organ sends a morbid impression to the brain,
it no longer does its work there in silence and self-sup-
pression, but asserts itself in an unwonted affection of
consciousness. The hypochondriac cannot withdraw his
attention from the morbid sensation to which it is irresistibly attracted, and which it aggravates; his interest in
all things else is gradually quenched, and his ability to
think and act freely in the relations of life sapped. The
step from this state to positive insanity is not a great one :
the strange and distressing sensation, being so anomalous,
so unlike anything of which the patient has had experience, affecting him so powerfully and so unaccountably,

gets at last an interpretation that seems suited to its extraordinary character; and he then imagines that some animal or man or devil has got inside him and is tormenting him. He has now a hallucination of the organic sense which dominates his thoughts, and he is truly insane. Not long since I saw a patient who believed that he had a man in his belly : when his bowels were constipated, the delusion became active, he made desperate efforts by vomiting to get rid of his tormentor, and was then surly, morose, and dangerous; but when his bowels had been relieved, the delusion subsided into the background, and he was good-tempered and industrious. If a patient, instead of attributing his sufferings to an absurdly impossible cause, ascribes them to a serious internal disease which he certainly has not got, there will be a difficulty in deciding whether he is insane or not, should he do injury to himself or others, as hypochondriacal melancholics sometimes do. It is a probable surmise that in those cases of insanity in which there are such delusions as that food will not enter the stomach, that there is no digestion, that the intestines are sealed up, there is a cause in a morbid irritation ascending from the viscera to the brain. I am furthermore disposed to think that a form of fearful melancholia in which the patient evinces an extreme morbid sensitiveness to his every thought, feeling, and act, in which he is, as it were, hypochondriacally distressed about whatever he thinks, feels, and does, imagining it, however trivial and innocent, to be a great sin, which has cost him his happiness in time and eternity, has its foundation in certain morbid states

of abdominal sensation. In cases of this sort, the delusion is not the cause of the feeling of despair, but is, as
it were, a condensation from it, and an attempted interpretation of it. The same thing is observed in dreams :
the images and events of a distressing dream are not the
causes of the feelings, but are caused by them ; they undergo strange and sudden metamorphoses without causing
much or any surprise, and they disappear together with
the terror the moment we awake, which would not be the
case if they really caused the terror.   We perceive, indeed,
in this generation of the image out of the feeling, the demonstration of the true nature of ghosts and apparitions ;
the nervous system being in an excited state of expectant
fear, and the images being the effects and exponents of
the feeling : they give the vague terror form.   Accordingly, as Coleridge has remarked, those who see a ghost
under such circumstances do not suffer much in consequence, though in telling the story they will perhaps say
that their hair stood on end, and that they were in an
agony of terror; whereas those who have been really
frightened by a figure dressed up as a ghost have often
suffered seriously from the shock, having fainted, or had
a fit, or gone mad.   In like manner, if an insane person
actually saw the dreadful things which he imagines that
he sees sometimes, and really thought the terrible thoughts
which he imagines he thinks, he would suffer in health
more than he does, if he did not actually die of them.

I come now to the thoracic organs. The heart and
the lungs are closely connected in their functions, so that
they mutually affect one another. Some diseases of the

lungs greatly oppress and trouble the heart; yet there is
reason to believe they have their special effects upon the
mind. How, indeed, can we think otherwise when we
contrast the sanguine confidence of the consumptive
patient with the anxious fear and apprehension exhibited
in some diseases of the heart? It used to be said that
disease of the heart was more frequent among the insane
than among the sane; but the latest observations do not
afford any support to the opinion, nor do they furnish
valid grounds to connect a particular variety of insanity
with heart-disease in those cases in which it does exist.
All that we are thus far warranted in affirming is, that if
there be a characteristic mental effect of such disease,
it is a great fear, mounting up at times to despairing
anguish; and perhaps I may venture to add, that if there
be a variety of mental disorder specifically connected
with heart-disease, it is that form of melancholia in which
the patient is overwhelmed with a vague and vast apprehension, where there is not so much a definite delusion
as a dreadful fear of everything actual and possible, and
which is sometimes described as *panphobia.*

 There has long been an opinion, which seems to be
well founded, that tubercle of the lungs is more common
among the insane than among the sane. For although
the proportion of deaths in asylums attributed to phthisis
is one-fourth, which is the same proportion as that for
the sane population above fourteen years of age, Dr.
Clouston has shown, by careful scrutiny of the records of
282 post-mortem examinations made in the Edinburgh
Asylum, that phthisis was the assigned cause of death in

only a little more than half of the cases in which there
was tubercle in the body. The symptoms of phthisis are
so much masked in the insane, there being usually no
cough and no expectoration, that its diagnosis is difficult,
and it is not always detected during life. The relation
between it and insanity has been noticed by several
writers : Schröder van der Kolk was distinctly of opinion that a hereditary predisposition to phthisis might
predispose to, or develop into, insanity, and, on the
other hand, that insanity predisposed to phthisis ; and Dr.
Clouston found that hereditary predisposition to insanity
existed in 7 per cent. more of the insane who were
tubercular than of the insane generally. When family
degeneration is far gone, the two diseases appear to occur
frequently, and the last member is likely to die insane
or phthisical, or both ; whether, therefore, they mutually
predispose to one another or not, they are often concomi-
tant effects in the course of degeneration. However,
in weighing the specific value of these observations, we
must not forget that, independently of any special relation, the enfeebled nutrition of tuberculosis will tend to
stimulate into activity the latent predisposition to insanity ; and that, in like manner, insanity, especially in
its melancholic forms, will favour the actual development of a predisposition to phthisis.

In the cases in which the development of phthisis and
insanity has been nearly contemporaneous, which are
about one-fourth of the cases in which they coexist, the
mental symptoms are of so peculiar and uniform a character as to have led to the inclusion of the cases in a

natural group under the designation of *phthisical mania.*
They have no positively distinctive symptom, it is true ;
they cannot be separated from other cases by a well-
defined line of demarcation.   Yet they do exhibit, Dr.
Clouston believes, certain common and uniform characters which justify their description as a separate variety.
They often begin in an insidious way by irritability, way-
wardness, and capriciousness of conduct, and apparent
weakening of intellect ; yet the patient converses ration-
ally when he chooses to talk, and shows that he still has
his intellect, albeit there is a great disinclination to exert
it.   To sign a certificate of his insanity would be no easy
matter.   Or they begin with an acutely maniacal or
melancholic stage, which is, however, of very short duration, soon passing into a half-maniacal, half-demented
state.   If there be a single characteristic feature, it is a
monomania of suspicion.   As the disease advances, the
symptoms of dementia predominate ; but there are occa-
sional brief attacks of irritable excitement and fitful
flashes of intelligence.   And in these cases, more often
than in other cases, there occurs a momentary revival of
intelligence before death.   We shall the more readily
admit the special features of phthisical mania when we
call to mind that there is in most phthisical patients a
peculiar mental state ; and that brief attacks of temporary mania or delirium sometimes occur in the course
of phthisis.   The phthisical patient is irritable, fanciful,
unstable of purpose, brilliant, and imaginative, but wanting in calmness and repose, quick of insight, but without
depth and comprehension ; everything is fitful—fitful

energy, fitful projects, fitful flashes of imagination. The
hectic is in his thoughts and in his actions. The whims
and imaginings of his mind become almost wanderings
at times, his fancies almost delusions.

I have now said enough concerning the sympathetic
mental effects of disordered organs, not certainly to set
forth adequately their nature, but to show the essential
importance of a careful study of them. To complete the
exposition of the action of pathological sympathies on
mind, it would be necessary to trace out the close relations that there are between the organic feelings and the
different kinds of special sensibility,—between systemic
and sense consciousness. The digestive organs have a
close sympathy with the sense of taste, as we observe in
the bad taste accompanying indigestion, in the nausea
and vomiting which a nauseous taste may cause, and in
the avoidance of poisonous matter by animals. The
respiratory organs and the sense of smell are, ·in like
manner, sympathetically associated ; and there can be no
doubt that the sense of smell has special relations with
the sexual feeling. The state of the digestive organs
notably affects the general sensibility of the skin. Dis-
turbances of these physiological sympathies may become
the occasions of insane delusions. Digestive derangement, perverting the taste, will engender a delusion that
the food is poisoned. Disease of the respiratory organs
appears sometimes to produce disagreeable smells, which
are then perhaps attributed to objective causes, such as
the presence of a corpse in the room, or to gases mali-
ciously disseminated in it by fancied persecutors. In mania,

smell and taste are often grossly perverted, for the patient will devour, with seeming relish and avidity, dirt and garbage of the most offensive kind. Increase, diminution, or perversion of the sensibility of the skin, one or other of which is not uncommon among the insane, may undoubtedly be the cause of extravagant delusions. We hardly, indeed, realize how completely the mind is dependent upon the habit of its sensations. The man who has lost a limb can hardly be persuaded that he has lost it, so sensible is he of the accustomed feelings in it ; years after he has lost it he dreams of vivid sensations and of active movements in it,—has, in fact, both sensory and motor hallucinations. It is easy, then, to understand how greatly abnormal sensations may perplex and deceive the unsound mind. A woman under Esquirol's care had complete anæsthesia of the skin : she believed that the devil had carried off her body. A soldier who was wounded at the battle of Austerlitz lost the sensibility of his skin, and from that time thought himself dead. When asked how he was, he replied, "Lambert no longer lives ; a cannon-ball carried him away at Austerlitz. What you see is not Lambert, but a badly imitated machine," which he always spoke of as *it*. A patient under my care, who suffered from general paralysis, and had lost sensibility and voluntary power of one side, could never be persuaded that another patient, a very harmless fellow, had not got hold of him, and was keeping him down ; and when convulsions occurred in the paralysed side, as they did from time to time, he swore terribly at his fancied tormentor. Were a sane person to wake up some morning with the cutaneous sensibility gone, or with a large area of it sending up to the brain perverted and quite unaccountable impressions, it might be a hard matter perhaps for him to help going mad.

The mental effects of perverted sensation afford a promising field for future research; when better understood it cannot be doubted that they will explain many phenomena in the pathology of mind that now quite baffle explanation. It behoves us to clearly realize the broad fact, which has most wide-reaching consequences in mental physiology and pathology, that all parts of the body, the highest and the lowest, have a sympathy with one another more intelligent than conscious intelligence can yet, or perhaps ever will, conceive; that there is not an organic motion, visible or invisible, sensible or insensible, ministrant to the noblest or to the most humble purposes, which does not work its appointed effect in the complex recesses of mind; that the mind, as the crowning achievement of organization, and the consummation and outcome of all its energies, really comprehends the bodily life.

I had originally set down within the purpose of these Lectures the consideration, which I must now forego, of the influence of the quantity and quality of the blood in the production of insanity. Poverty and vitiation of blood may certainly play a weighty part in producing mental, as they do in producing other nervous disorders. Lower the supply of blood to the brain below a certain level, and the power of thinking is abolished; the brain will then no more do mental work than a waterwheel will move the machinery of the mill when the water is lowered so as not to touch it. When a strong emotion produces a temporary loss of consciousness, it is to be presumed that a contraction of arteries takes place within the brain similar to that which causes the pallor of the face; and when the labouring heart pumps hard to overcome the obstruction, and the walls of the vessels are weak, they may burst, and the patient die of effusion of blood. During sleep the supply of blood to the brain is lessened naturally, and we perceive the effects of the lowering of the supply, as it takes place, in the sort of incoherence or mild delirium of ideas just before falling off to sleep. To a like condition of things we ought most probably to attribute the attacks of transitory mania or delirium that occur now and then in consequence of great physical exhaustion, as from great and sudden loss of blood, or just as convalescence from fever or other acute disease is setting in, or in the prostration of phthisis, and which a glass of wine opportunely given will sometimes cure. The distress of the melancholic patient is greatest when he wakes in the morning, which is a time when a watch ought to be kept specially over the suicidal patient; the reason lying probably in the effects of the diminished cerebral circulation during sleep.

If the state of the blood be vitiated by reason of some poison bred in the body, or introduced into it from without, the mental functions may be seriously deranged. We are able, indeed, by means of the drugs at our command, to perform all sorts of experiments on the mind: we can suspend its action for a time by chloral or chloro-

form, can exalt its functions by small doses of opium or
moderate doses of alcohol, can pervert them, producing
an artificial delirium, by the administration of large enough
doses of belladonna and Indian hemp. We can positively
do more experimentally with the functions of the mind-
centres than we can do with those of any other organ of
the body. When these are exalted in consequence of a
foreign substance introduced into the blood, it cannot be
doubted that some *physical* effect is produced on the
nerve-element, which is the condition of the increased
activity, not otherwise probably than as happens when a
fever makes, as it certainly will sometimes do, a demented
person, whose mind seemed gone past all hope of even
momentary recovery, quite sensible for the time being.
Perhaps this should teach us that just as there are vibrations of light which we cannot see, and vibrations of sound
which we cannot hear, so there are molecular movements
in the brain which are incapable of producing thought
ordinarily, not sufficing to affect consciousness, but which
may do so when the sensibility of the molecules is exalted by physical or chemical modification of them.

Alcohol yields us, in its direct effects, the abstract and
brief chronicle of the course of mania. At first there
is an agreeable excitement, a lively flow of ideas, a
revival of old ideas and feelings which seemed to have
passed from the mind, a general increase of mental
activity—a condition very like that which often precedes
an attack of acute mania, when the patient is witty,
lively, satirical, makes jokes or rhymes, and certainly
exhibits a brilliancy of fancy which he is capable of at

no other time.   Then there follows, in the next stage of
its increasing action, as there does in mania, the automatic excitation of ideas which start up and follow one
another without order, so that thought and speech are
more or less incoherent, while passion is easily excited.
After this stage has lasted for a time, in some longer,
in others shorter, it passes into one of depression and
maudlin melancholy, just as mania sometimes passes into
melancholia, or convulsion into paralysis.   And the last
stage of all is one of stupor and dementia.   If the abuse
of alcohol be continued for years, it may cause different
forms of mental derangement, in each of which the muscular are curiously like the mental symptoms : delirium
tremens in one, an acute noisy and destructive mania in
another, chronic alcoholism in a third, and a condition
of mental weakness with loss of memory and loss of
energy in a fourth.

    Writers on gout agree that a suppressed gout may
entail mental derangement in some persons ; and, on the
other hand, that insanity has sometimes disappeared with
the appearance of the usual gouty paroxysm.   Sydenham
noticed and described a species of mania supervening
on an epidemic of intermittent fever, which, he remarks,
contrary to all other kinds of madness, would not yield
to plentiful venesection and purging.   Griesinger, again,
has directed attention to cases in which, instead of the
usual symptoms of ague, the patient has had an intermittent insanity in regular tertian or quartan attacks, and
has been cured by quinine.   We must bear in mind,
however, that intermittence may be a feature of insanity

as of other nervous diseases, without ague having anything whatever to do with it, and without quinine doing
any good whatever.   Quinine will not cure the intermittence of nervous diseases, though it may cure ague in
which the symptoms are intermittent.   Griesinger has
also pointed out that mental disorder has sometimes
occurred in the course of acute rheumatism, the swelling
of the joints meanwhile subsiding.   These facts, with
others which I cannot dwell upon now, prove how important an agency in the production of insanity a perverted
state of the blood may be.   But it is a mode of causation
of which we know so little that I may justly declare we
know next to nothing.   The observation and classification
of mental disorders has been so exclusively psychological
that we have not sincerely realized the fact that they illustrate the same pathological principles as other diseases,
are produced in the same way, and must be investigated
in the same spirit of positive research.   Until this be
done I see no hope of improvement in our knowledge of
them, and no use in multiplying books about them.

It is quite true that when we have referred all the cases
of insanity which we can to bodily causes, and grouped
them according to their characteristic body and mental
features, there will remain cases which we cannot refer
to any recognizable bodily cause or connect with any
definite bodily disease, and which we must be content to
describe as *idiopathic*.   The explanation of these cases
we shall probably discover ultimately in the influence of
the hereditary neurosis and in the peculiarities of individual temperament.   It is evident that there are funda-

mental differences of temperament, and it is furthermore
plain that different natures will be differently favoured in
the struggle of existence ; one person will have an advantage over another, and by the operation of the law of
Natural Selection there will be a success of the fittest to
succeed.   It is with the development of mind in the
conduct of life as it is with every form of life in its relation to its environment.   Life is surrounded by forces
that are always tending to destroy it, and with which it
may be represented as in a continued warfare ; so long
as it contends successfully with them, winning from them
and constraining them to further its development, it
flourishes ; but when it can no longer strive, when they
succeed in winning from it and increasing at its expense,
it begins to decay and die.   So it is with mind in the
circumstances of its existence : the individual who cannot use circumstances, or accommodate himself successfully to them, and in the one way or the other make
them further his development, is controlled and used
by them ; being weak, he must be miserable, must be a
victim ; and one way in which his suffering and failure
will be manifest will be in insanity.   Thus it is that
mental trials which serve in the end to strengthen a
strong nature break down a weak one which cannot fitly
react, and that the efficiency of a moral cause of insanity
betrays a conspiracy from within with the unfavourable
outward circumstances.

It behoves us to bear distinctly in mind, when we take
the moral causes of insanity into consideration, that the
mental suffering or psychical pain of a sad emotion testi-

fies to actual wear and tear of nerve-element, to disintegration of some kind ; it is the exponent of a *physical* change.   What the change is we know not ; but we may take it to be beyond question that, when a shock imparted to the mind through the senses causes a violent emotion, it produces a real commotion in the molecules of the brain.   It is not that an intangible something flashes inwards and mysteriously affects an intangible metaphysical entity ; but that an impression made on the sense is conveyed along nervous paths of communication, and produces a definite physical effect in physically constituted mind-centres ; and that the mental effect, which is the exponent of the physical change, may be then transferred by molecular motion to the muscles, thus getting muscular expression, or to the processes of nutrition and secretion, getting expression in modifications of them. When there is a native infirmity or instability of nerve-element, in consequence of bad ancestral influences, the individual will be more liable to, and will suffer more from, such violent mental commotions; the disintegrating change in the nerve-element will be more likely to pass into a disorganization which rest and nutrition cannot repair, not otherwise than as happens with the elements of any other organ under like conditions of excessive stimulation.   As physicians, we cannot afford to lose sight of the physical aspects of mental states, if we would truly comprehend the nature of mental disease, and learn to treat it with success.   The metaphysician may, for the purposes of speculation, separate mind from body, and evoke the laws of its operation out of the depths of self-

consciousness ; but the physician—who has to deal practically with the thoughts, feelings, and conduct of men ;
who has to do with mind, not as an abstract entity concerning which he may be content to speculate, but as a
force in nature, the operations of which he must patiently
observe and anxiously labour to influence—must recognize
how entirely the integrity of the mental fuuctions depends
on the integrity of the bodily organization—must acknowledge the essential unity of body and mind.

To set forth this unity has been a chief aim in these
Lectures, because I entertain a most sincere conviction
that a just conception of it must lie at the foundation of
a real advance in our knowledge both of the physiology
and pathology of mind. I have no wish whatever to
exalt unduly the body ; I have, if possible, still less desire
to degrade the mind ; but I do protest with all the energy
I dare use against the unjust and most unscientific practice of declaring the body vile and despicable, of looking
down upon the highest and most wonderful contrivance
of creative skill as something of which man dare venture
to feel ashamed. I cannot now summarize the facts and
arguments which I have brought forward ; I must trust
to the indulgence of your memory of them when I declare
that to my mind it appears a clear scientific duty to repudiate the quotation from an old writer, which the late
Sir William Hamilton used to hang on the wall of his
lecture-room :—

> " On earth there is nothing great but man,
> In man there is nothing great but mind."

The aphorism, which, like most aphorisms, contains an

equal measure of truth and of untruth, is suitable enough
to the pure metaphysician, but it is most unsuitable to
the scientific inquirer, who is bound to reject it, not
because of that which is not true in it only, but much
more because of the baneful spirit with which it is
inspired. On earth there are assuredly other things
great besides man, though none greater; and in man
there are other things great besides mind, though none
greater. And whosoever, inspired with the spirit of the
aphorism, thinks to know anything truly of man without
studying most earnestly the things on earth that lead up
to man, or to know anything truly of mind without studying most earnestly the things in the body that lead up to
and issue in mind, will enter on a barren labour, which,
if not a sorrow to himself, will assuredly be sorrow and
vexation of spirit to others. To reckon the highest
operations of mind to be functions of a mental organization is to exalt, not to degrade, our conception of
creative power and skill. For if it be lawful and right
to burst into admiration of the wonderful contrivance in
nature by which noble and beautiful products are formed
out of base materials, it is surely much stronger evidence
of contrivance to have developed the higher mental
functions by evolution from the lower, and to have used
forms of matter as the organic instruments of all. I
know not why the Power which created matter and its
properties should be thought not to have endowed it
with the functions of reason, feeling, and will, seeing that
whether we discover it to be so endowed or not, the
mystery is equally incomprehensible to us, equally simple

and easy to the Power which created matter and its properties. To a right-thinking and right-feeling mind the
beauty, the grandeur, the mystery of Nature are augmented,
not lessened, by each new glimpse into the secret recesses
of her operations. The sun going forth from its chamber
in the east to run its course is not less glorious in majesty
because we have discovered the law of gravitation, and
are able by spectral analysis to detect the metals which
enter into its composition—because it is no longer Helios
driving his golden chariot through the pathless spaces of
the heavens. The mountains are not less imposing in
their grandeur because the Oreads have deserted them,
nor the groves less attractive, the streams more desolate,
because science has banished the Dryads and the Naiads.
No, science has not destroyed poetry, nor expelled the
Divine from nature, but has furnished the materials, and
given the presages, of a higher poetry and a mightier
philosophy than the world has yet seen. The grave of
each superstition which it slays is the womb of a better
birth. And if it come to pass in its onward march—as
it may well be it will come to pass—that other super-
stitions shall be dethroned as the sun-god has been
dethroned, we may rest assured that this also will be a
step in human progress, and in the beneficent evolution
of the Power which ruleth alike the courses of the stars
and the ways of men.

APPENDIX.

1. THE LIMITS OF PHILOSOPHICAL INQUIRY.

2. THE THEORY OF VITALITY.

THE

LIMITS OF PHILOSOPHICAL INQUIRY.[1]

IT is not a little hard upon those who now devote
themselves to the patient interrogation of nature, by
means of observation and experiment, that they should
be counted, whether they will or not, ministers of the
so-called Positive Philosophy, and disciples of him who
is popularly considered the founder of that philosophy.
No matter that positive investigation within the limits
which Comte prescribes was pursued earnestly and systematically before his advent, and with an exactness of
method of which he had no conception ; that many of
those distinguished since his time for their scientific researches and generalizations have been unacquainted with
his writings ; that others who have studied them withhold
their adherence from his doctrines, or energetically disclaim them. These things are not considered ; so soon
as a scientific inquirer pushes his researches into the

[1] JOURNAL OF MENTAL SCIENCE, No. 70. The Limits of
Philosophical Inquiry. Address delivered to the Members of the
Edinburgh Philosophical Institution, November 6, 1868. By
William, Lord Archbishop of York. (Edmonston and Douglas.)

phenomena of life and mind, he is held to be a Comtist. Thus it happens that there is a growing tendency in the public mind to identify modern science with the Positive Philosophy. Considering how much mischief has often been done by identifying the character of an epoch of thought with the doctrines of some eminent man who has lived and laboured and taken the lead in it, and thus making his defects and errors, hardened into formulas, chains to fetter the free course of thought, it is no wonder that scientific men should be anxious to disclaim Comte as their lawgiver, and to protest against such a king being set up to reign over them. Not conscious of any personal obligation to his writings, conscious how much, in some respects, he has misrepresented the spirit and pretensions of science, they repudiate the allegiance which his enthusiastic disciples would force upon them, and which popular opinion is fast coming to think a natural one. They do well in thus making a timely assertion of independence ; for if it be not done soon, it will soon be too late to be done well. When we look back at the history of systems of religion and philosophy, it is almost appalling to reflect how entirely one man has appropriated the intellectual development of his age, and how despotically he has constrained the faith of generations after him ; the mind of mankind is absolutely oppressed by the weight of his authority, and his errors and limitations are deemed not less sacred than the true ideas of which he has been the organ : for a time he is made an idol, at the sound of whose name the human intellect is expected to fall down and worship, as the people, nations, and languages were expected, at what time they heard the sound of the flute, harp, sackbut, dulcimer, and all kinds of music, to fall down and worship the golden image which Nebuchadnezzar the king had set up. Happily it is not so easy to take captive the understanding now, when thought is busy on so many subjects in such various domains of nature, and when an army of investigators often marches where formerly a solitary pioneer painfully sought his way, as it was when the fields of intellectual activity were few and limited, and the labourers in them few also.

A lecture delivered by the Archbishop of York before the Edinburgh Philosophical Institution, which has been published as a pamphlet, contains a plain, earnest, and on the whole temperate, but not very closely reasoned, criticism, from his point of view, of the tendency of modern scientific research, or rather of Positivism, and a somewhat vague declaration of the limits of philosophical inquiry. He perceives with sorrow, but not with great apprehension, that the prospects of philosophy are clouded over in England, France, and Germany, and that a great part of the thinking world is occupied with physical researches. But he does not therefore despair ; believing that Positivism indicates only a temporary mood, produced by prostration and lassitude after a period of unusual controversy, and that it will after a time pass away, and be followed by a new era of speculative activity. It may be presumed that men, weary of their fruitless efforts to scale the lofty and seemingly barren heights of true philosophy, have taken the easy path of Positivism, which does not lead upwards at all, but leads, if it be followed far enough, to quagmires of unbelief. The facts on which the Archbishop bases his opinion, and the steps of reasoning by which he is able thus to couple a period of speculative activity with a period of religious belief, and to declare a system of positive scientific research to be linked inseparably with a system of unbelief, do not appear; they are sufficient to inspire strong conviction in him, but they apparently lie too far down in the depths of his moral consciousness to be capable of being unfolded, in lucid sequence, to the apprehension of others.

To the critical reader of the lecture it must at once occur that a want of discrimination between things that are widely different is the cause of no little looseness, if not recklessness, of assertion. In the first place, the Archbishop identifies off-hand the course and aim of modern scientific progress with the Positivism of Comte and his followers. This is very much as if any one should insist on attributing the same character and the same aim to persons who were travelling for a considerable distance along the same road. As it was Comte's great aim to organize an harmonious co-ordination and subordination of the sciences, he assimilated and used for his purpose the scientific knowledge which was available to him, and systematized the observed method of scientific progress from the more simple and general to the more special and complex studies ; but it assuredly is most unwarrantable to declare those who are engaged in physical research to be committed to his conclusions and pretensions, and there can be no question that a philosophy of science, when it is written, will differ widely from the so-called Positive Philosophy.

In the second place, the Archbishop unwittingly perpetrates a second and similarly reckless injustice in assuming, as he does, that modern science must needs accept what he describes as the sensational philosophy. " Thus the business of science," he says, " is to gather up the facts as they appear, without addition or perversion of the senses. As the senses are our only means of knowledge, and we can only know things as they present themselves to the eye and ear, it follows that our know-ledge is not absolute knowledge of the things, but a knowledge of their relations to us, that is, of our sensations." Passing by the question, which might well be raised, whether any one, even the founder of the sensational philosophy, ever thus crudely asserted the senses to be our only means of knowledge, and our knowledge to be only a knowledge of our sensations ; passing by, too, any discussion concerning what the Archbishop means, if he means anything, by an absolute knowledge of things as distinct from a knowledge of things in their relations to us, and all speculations con-cerning the faculties which finite and relative beings who are not archbishops have of apprehending and compre-hending the absolute ; it is necessary to protest against the assumption that science is committed to such a representation of the sensational philosophy, or to the sensational philosophy at all. Those modern inquirers who have pushed farthest their physical researches into mental functions and bodily organs, have notoriously been at great pains to discriminate between the nervous centres which minister to sensation and those which minister to reflection, and have done much to elucidate the physical and functional connections between them. They have never been guilty of calling all knowledge a knowledge only of sensations, for they recognize how vague, barren, and unmeaning are the terms of the old language of philosophical strife, when an attempt is made to apply them with precision to the phenomena revealed by exact scientific observation. The sensorial centres with which the senses are in direct connection are quite distinct from, and subordinate to, the nervous centres of ideation or reflection—the supreme hemispherical ganglia. It is in these, which are far more developed in man than in any other animal, and more developed in the higher than in the lower races of men, that sensation is transformed into knowledge, and that reflective consciousness has its seat. The knowledge so acquired is not drained from the outer world through the senses, nor is it a physical mixture or a chemical compound of so much received from without and so much added by the mind or brain; it is an organized result of a most complex and delicate process of development in the highest kind of organic element in nature—a mental organization accomplished, like any other organization, in accordance with definite laws. We have to do with *laws of life*, and the language used in the interpretation of phenomena must accord with ideas derived from the study of organization; for assuredly it cannot fail to produce confusion if it be the expression only of ideas derived from the laws of physical phenomena, so far as these are at present known to us. Now the organization of a definite sensation is a very different matter from, has no resemblance in nature to, the physical impression made upon the organ of sense, and the organization of an idea is a higher and more complex vital process than the organization of a sensation; to call knowledge, therefore, a knowledge only of sensation is either a meaningless proposition, or, in so far as it has meaning, it is falser than it would be to affirm the properties of a chemical compound to be those of its constituents. Were they who pursue the scientific study of mind not more thoughtful than the Archbishop of York gives them credit for being, they would have no reason to give why animals with as many senses as man has, and with some of them more acute than his, have not long since attained, like him, to an understanding of the benefits of establishing arch-bishoprics.

It must be understood that by the assertion of the organic basis of mental function is not meant that the mind imposes the laws of its own organization; on the contrary, it obeys them, knowing not whence they come nor whither they tend. Innate ideas, fundamental ideas, categories of the understanding, and like metaphysical expressions, are obscure intimations of the laws of action of the internal organizing power under the conditions of its existence and exercise; and it is easy to perceive that a new and higher sense conferred on man, altering entirely these conditions, would at once render necessary a new

order of fundamental ideas or categories of the understanding.   That all our knowledge is relative cannot be
denied, unless it be maintained that in that wonderful
organizing power which cometh from afar there lies hidden
that which may be intuitively revealed to consciousness
as absolute knowledge—that the nature of the mysterious
power which inspires and impels evolution may, by a flash
of intuitive consciousness, be made manifest to the mind in
the process of its own development.   If nature be attain-
ing to a complete self-consciousness in man, far away
from such an end as it seems to be, it is conceivable that
this might happen ; and if such a miraculous inspiration
were thus to reveal the unknown, it would be a revelation
of the one primeval Power.   Clearly, however, as positive
scientific research is powerless before a vast mystery,—the
whence, what, and whither of the mighty power which
gives the impulse to evolution,—it is not justified in
making any proposition regarding it.   This, however, it
may rightly do ; while keeping its inquiries within the
limits of the knowable, it may examine critically, and use
all available means of testing, the claims and credentials
of any professed revelation of the mystery.   And it is in
the pursuit of such inquiries that it would have been
satisfactory to have had from the Archbishop, as a high
priest of the mystery, some gleam of information as to the
proper limits which he believes ought to be observed.   At
what point is the hitherto and no farther to which inquiry
may advance in that direction ?   Where do we reach the
holy ground when it becomes necessary to put the scientific shoes from off our feet ?   There must assuredly be

some right and duty of examination into the evidence of revelations claiming to be Divine; for if it were not so, how could the intelligent Mussulman ever be, if he ever is, persuaded to abandon the one God of his faith, and to accept what must seem to him the polytheism of the Christian Trinity?

Another error, or rather set of errors, into which the Archbishop plunges, is that he assumes positive science to be materialistic, and materialism to involve the negation of God, of immortality, and of free will. This imputation of materialism, which ought never to have been so lightly made, it is quite certain that the majority of scientific men would earnestly disclaim. Moreover, the materialist, as such, is not under any logical constraint whatever to deny either the existence of a God, or the immortality of the soul, or free will. One is almost tempted to say that in two things the Archbishop distances competition: first, in the facility with which he loses or dispenses with the links of his own chain of reasoning; and, secondly, in his evident inability to perceive, when looking sincerely with all his might, real and essential distinctions which are at all subtile, which are not broadly, and almost coarsely, marked. If the edge of a distinction be fine, if it be not as blunt as a weaver's beam, it fails seemingly to attract his attention. Whosoever believes sincerely in the doctrine of the resurrection of the body, as taught by the Apostle Paul, which all Christians profess to do, must surely have some difficulty in conceiving the immortality of the soul apart from that of the body; for if the Apostle's preaching and the

Christian's faith be not vain, and the body do rise again, then it may be presumed that the soul and it will share a common immortality, as they have shared a common mortality. So far, then, from materialism being the negation of immortality, the greatest of the apostles, the great Apostle of the Gentiles, earnestly preached materialism as essential to the life which is to come. There is as little or less justification for saying that materialism involves of necessity the denial of free will. The facts on which the doctrine of free will is based are the same facts of observation, whether spiritualism or materialism be the accepted faith, and the question of their interpretation is not essentially connected with the one or the other faith ; the spiritualist may consistently deny, and the materialist consistently advocate, free will. In like manner, the belief in the existence of God is nowise inconsistent with the most extreme materialism, for the belief is quite independent of the facts and reasons on which that faith is founded. The spiritualist may deny God the power to make matter think, but the materialist need not deny the existence of God because he holds that matter may be capable of thought. Multitudes may logically believe that mind is inseparable from body in life or death—that it is born with it, grows, ripens, decays, and dies with it, without disbelieving in a great and intelligent Power who has called man into being, and ordained the greater light to rule the day and the lesser light to rule the night.

What an unnecessary horror hangs over the word materialism ! It has an ugly sound, and an indefinite meaning, and is well suited, therefore, to be set up as a sort of moral scarecrow; but if it be closely examined, it will be found to have the semblance of something terrible, and to be empty of any real harm. In the assertion that mind is altogether a function of matter, there is no more actual irreverence than in asserting that matter is the realization of mind; the one and the other proposition being equally meaningless so far as they postulate a knowledge of anything more than phenomena. Whether extension be visible thought, or thought invisible extension, is a question of a choice of words, and not of a choice of conceptions. To those who cannot conceive that any organization of matter, however complex, should be capable of such exalted functions as those which are called mental, is it really more conceivable that any organization of matter can be the mechanical instrument of the complex manifestations of an immaterial mind? Is it not as easy for an omnipotent power to endow matter with mental functions as it is to create an immaterial entity capable of accomplishing them through matter? Is the Creator's arm shortened, so that He cannot endow matter with sensation and ideation? It is strangely overlooked by many who write on this matter, that the brain is not a dead instrument, but a living organ, with functions of a higher kind than those of any other bodily organ, insomuch as its organic nature and structure far surpass those of any other organ. What, then, are those functions if they are not mental? No one thinks it necessary to assume an immaterial liver behind the hepatic structure, in order to account for its functions. But so far as the nature of nerve and the complex structure of the cerebral convolutions exceed in dignity the hepatic elements and structure, so far must the material functions of the brain exceed those of the liver. Men are not sufficiently careful to ponder the wonderful operations of which matter is capable, or to reflect on the miracles effected by it which are continually before their eyes. Are the properties of a chemical compound less mysterious essentially because of the familiarity with which we handle them? Consider the seed dropped into the ground : it swells with germinating energy, bursts its integuments, sends upwards a delicate shoot, which grows into a stem, putting forth in due season its leaves and flowers, until finally a beautiful structure is formed, such as Solomon in all his glory could not equal, and all the art of mankind cannot imitate. And yet all these processes are operations of matter; for it is not thought necessary to assume an immaterial or spiritual plant which effects its purposes through the agency of the material structure which we observe. Surely there are here exhibited properties of matter wonderful enough to satisfy any one of the powers that may be inherent in it. Are we, then, to believe that the highest and most complex development of organic structure is not capable of even more wonderful operations? Would you have the human body, which is a microcosm containing all the forms and powers of matter organized in the most delicate and complex manner, to possess lower powers than those forms of matter exhibit separately in nature? Trace the gradual development of the nervous system through the animal series, from its first germ to its most complex evolution, and let it be declared at what point it suddenly loses all its inherent properties as living structure and becomes the mere mechanical instrument of a spiritual entity. In what animal or in what class of animals does the immaterial principle abruptly intervene and supersede the agency of matter, becoming the entirely distinct cause of a similar, though more exalted, order of mental phenomena? To appeal to the consciousness of every man for the proof of a power within him totally distinct from any function of the body, is not admissible as an argument, while it is admitted that consciousness can make no observation of the bodily organ and its functions, and until therefore it be proved that matter, even when in the form of the most complex organization, is incapable of certain mental functions. Why may it not, indeed, be capable of consciousness, seeing that, whether it be or not, the mystery is equally incomprehensible to us, and must be reckoned equally simple and easy to the Power which created matter and its properties? When again we are told that every part of the body is in a constant state of change, that within a certain period every particle of it is renewed, and yet that amidst these changes a man feels that he remains essentially the same, we perceive nothing inconsistent with the idea of the action of a material organ; for it is not absurd to suppose that in the brain the new series of particles take the pattern of those which they replace, as they do in other organs and tissues which are continually changing their substance yet preserve their identity. Even the scar of a wound on the finger is not often effaced, but grows as the body grows : why, then, assume the necessity of an immaterial principle to prevent the impression of an idea from being lost?

The truth is that men have disputed vaguely and violently about matter and motion, and about the impossibility of matter affecting an immaterial mind, never having been at the pains to reflect carefully upon the different kinds of matter and the corresponding differences of kind in its motions. All sorts of matter, diverse as they are, were vaguely *matter*—there was no discrimination made ; and all the manifold and special properties of matter were comprised under the general term *motion*. This was not, nor could it lead to, good ; for matter really rises in dignity from physical matter in which physical properties exist to chemical matter and chemical forces, and from chemical matter to living matter and its modes of force ; and then in the scale of life a continuing ascent leads from the lowest kind of living matter with its force or energy, through different kinds of physiological elements with their special energies or functions, to the highest kind of living matter with its force—viz., nerve matter and nerve force ; and, lastly, through the different kinds of nerve-cells and their energies to the most exalted agents of mental function. Obviously then simple ideas derived from observation of mechanical phenomena cannot fitly be applied to the explanation of the functions of that most complex combination of elements and energies, physical and chemical, in a small space, which we have in living structure ; to speak of mechanical vibration in nerves and nerve-centres is to convey false ideas of their extremely delicate and complex energies, and thus seriously to hinder the formation of more just conceptions.

In like manner, much barren discussion has been owing to the undiscriminating inclusion of all kinds of mental manifestations under the vague and general term *mind;* for there are most important differences in the nature and dignity of so-called mental phenomena, when they are properly observed and analysed. Those who have not been at the pains to follow the order of development of mental phenomena and to make themselves acquainted with the different kinds of functions that concur to form what we call mental action, and who have not studied the differences of matter, are doing no better than beating the air when they declaim against materialism. By rightly submitting the understanding to facts, it is made evident that, on the one hand, matter rises in dignity and function until its energies merge insensibly into functions which are described as mental, and, on the other hand, that there are gradations of mental function, the lowest of which confessedly do not transcend the functions of matter. The burden of proving that the *Deus ex machinâ* of a spiritual entity intervenes somewhere, and where it intervenes, clearly lies upon those who make the assertion or whó need the hypothesis. They are not justified in arbitrarily fabricating an hypothesis entirely inconsistent with experience of the orderly development of nature, which even postulates a domain of nature that human senses cannot take any cognizance of, and in then calling upon those who reject their assumption to disprove

K

it. These have done enough if they show that there are no grounds for and no need of the hypothesis.

Here we might properly take leave of the Archbishop's address, were it not that the looseness of his statements and the way in which his understanding is governed by the old phrases of philosophical disputes tempt further criticism, and make it a duty to expose aspects of the subject of which he does not evince the least apprehension. He would, we imagine, be hard put to it to support the heavy indictment contained in the following sentence which he flings off as he goes heedlessly forward :—"A system which pretends to dispense with the ideas of God, of immortality, of free agency, of causation, and of design, would seem to offer few attractions." The question of the value of any system of philosophy is not, it may be observed incidentally, whether it is unattractive because it dispenses with received notions, still less because its adversaries imagine that it must dispense with them ; but it is whether it possesses that degree of fundamental truth which will avail to enlarge the knowledge, and to attract ultimately the belief of mankind. History does not record that the doctrines of Christianity were found attractive by the philosophers of Greece or Rome when they were first preached there ; does, indeed, record that Paul preaching on Mars' Hill at Athens, the city of intellectual enlightenment, and declaring to the inhabitants the unknown God whom they ignorantly worshipped, made no impression, but found it prudent to depart thence to Corinth, nowise renowned at that time as a virtuous city, renowned, indeed, in far other wise. We have not, however, quoted the foregoing sentence in order to repudiate popular attractiveness as a criterion of truth, but to take occasion to declare the wide difference between the modest spirit of scientific inquiry and the confident dogmatism of the so-called Positive Philosophy. Science, recognizing the measure of what it can impart to be bounded by the existing limits of scientific inquiry, makes no proposition whatever concerning that which lies beyond these limits ; equally careful, on the one hand, to avoid a barren enunciation in words of what it cannot apprehend in thought, and, on the other hand, to refrain from a blind denial of possibilities transcending its means of research. A calm acquiescence in ignorance until light comes is its attitude. It must be borne clearly in mind, however, that this scrupulous care to abstain from presumptuous assertions does not warrant the imposition of any arbitrary barrier to the reach of its powers, but is quite consistent with the conviction of the possibility of an invasion and subjugation of the unknown to a practically unlimited extent, and with the most strenuous efforts to lessen its domain.

The wonder is—and the more it is considered the greater it seems—that human intelligence should ever have grown to the height either of affirming or of denying the existence of a God. Certainly the denial implies, even if the affirmation does not also, the assumption of the attributes of a God by him who makes it. Let imagination travel unrestrained through the immeasureable heavens, past the myriads of orbs which, revolving

K 2

in their appointed paths, constitute our solar system, through distances which words cannot express nor mind conceive definitely, to other suns and other planetary systems ; beyond these glimmer in the vast distance the lights of more solar systems, whose rays, extinguished in the void, never reach our planet : still they are not the end, for as thought in its flight leaves them behind, and they vanish in remote space, other suns appear, until, as the imagination strives to realize their immensity, the heavens seem almost an infinite void, so small a space do the scattered clusters of planets fill. Then let sober reflection take up the tale, and, remembering how small a part of the heavenly hosts our solar system is, and how small a part of our solar system the earth is, consider how entirely dependent man, and beast, and plant, and every living thing is upon the heat which this our planet receives from the sun ; how vegetation flourishes through its inspiring influence, and the vegetation of the past in long-buried forests gives up again the heat which ages ago it received from the sun ; how animal life is sustained by the life of the vegetable kingdom, and by the heat which is received directly from the sun ; and how man, as the crown of living things, and his highest mental energy, as the crown of his development, depend on all that has gone before him in the evolution of nature :— considering all these things, does not living nature appear but a small and incidental by-play of the sun's energies ? Seems it not an unspeakable presumption to affirm that man is the main end and purpose of creation ? Is it not appalling to think that he should dare to speak of what so far surpasses the reach of his feeble senses, and of the power which ordains and governs the order of events—impiously to deny the existence of a God, or not less impiously to create one in his image? The portion of the universe with which man is brought into relation by his existing sentiency is but a fragment, and to measure the possibilities of the infinite unknown by the standard of what he knows is very much as if the oyster should judge all nature by the experience gained within its shell—should deny the existence on earth of a human being, because its intelligence cannot conceive his nature or recognize his works. Encompassing us and transcending our ken is a universe of energies; how can man then, the "feeble atom of an hour," presume to affirm whose glory the heavens declare, whose handiwork the firmament showeth? Certainly true science does not so dogmatize.

Bacon, in a well-known and often-quoted passage, has remarked: "that a little philosophy inclineth men's minds to Atheism, but depth in philosophy bringeth men's minds about to religion; for while the mind of man looketh upon second causes scattered, it may sometimes rest in them, and go no further; but when it beholdeth the chain of them, confederate and linked together, it must needs fly to Providence and Deity." It is not easy to perceive, indeed, how modern science, which makes its inductions concerning natural forces from observation of their manifestations, and arrives at generalizations of different forces, can, after observation of nature, avoid the generalization of an intelligent mental force, linked in harmonious association and essential relations with other forces, but leading and constraining them to higher aims of evolution. To speak of such evolution as the course of nature is to endow an undefined agency with the properties which are commonly assigned to a god, whether it be called God or not. The nature, aim and power of this supreme intelligent force, working so far as we know from everlasting to everlasting, it is plainly impossible that man, a finite and transient part of nature, should comprehend. To suppose him capable of doing so would be to suppose him endowed with the very attributes which, having only in part himself, he ascribes in the whole to Deity.

Whether the low savage has or has not the idea of a God, is a question which seems hardly to deserve the amount of attention which it has received. It is certain that he feels himself surrounded and overruled by forces the natures and laws of which he is quite ignorant of, and that he is apt to interpret them, more or less clearly, as the work of some being of like passions with himself, but vastly more powerful, whom it is his interest to propitiate. Indeed, it would appear, so far as the information of travellers enables us to judge, that the idea entertained of God by the savage who has any such idea is nearly allied to that which civilized people have or have had of a devil; for it is the vague dread of a being whose delight is in bringing evil upon him rather than that of a being who watches over and protects him. Being ignorant altogether of the order of nature, and of

the fixed laws under which calamities and blessings alike
come, he frames a dim, vague, and terrible embodiment
of the causes of those effects which touch him most
painfully. Will it be believed, then, that the Archbishop
of York actually appeals to the instinct of the savage
to rebuke the alleged atheism of science? Let it be
granted, however, that the alleged instinct of the savage
points to a God and not to a devil ruling the world, it
must in all fairness be confessed that it is a dim, undefined, fearful idea—if that can be called an idea which
form has none—having no relationship to the conception
of a God which is cherished among civilized people.
In like manner as the idea of a devil has undergone a
remarkable development with the growth of intelligence
from age to age, until in some quarters there is evinced
a disposition to improve him out of being, so the conception of a God has undergone an important development through the ages, in correspondence with the
development of the human mind. The conceptions of
God affirmed by different revelations notably reflect, and
are an index of, the intellectual and moral character of
the people to whom each revelation has been made, and
the God of the same religion does unquestionably advance
with the mental evolution of the people professing it,
being differently conceived of at different stages of culture. Art, in its early infancy, when it is, so to speak,
learning its steps, endeavours to copy nature, and, copy-
ing it badly, exaggerates and caricatures it, whence the
savage's crude notion of a God ; but the aim and work
of the highest art is to produce by idealization the

illusion of a higher reality, whence a more exalted and spiritual conception of Deity.

Notwithstanding the Archbishop's charge of atheism against science, there is hardly one, if indeed there be even one, eminent scientific inquirer who has denied the existence of God, while there is notably more than one who has evinced a childlike simplicity of faith. The utmost claim of scientific scepticism is the right to examine the evidence of a revelation professing to be Divine, in the same searching way as it would examine any other evidence—to endeavour to trace the origin and development, and to weigh the value, of religious conceptions as of other conceptions. It violates the fundamental habit of the scientific mind, the very principle of its nature, to demand of it the unquestioning acceptance of any form of faith which tradition may hand down as divinely revealed. When the followers of a religion appeal, as the followers of every religion do, in proof of it, to the testimony of miraculous events contrary to the experience of the present order of nature, there is a scientific fact not contrary to experience of the order of nature which they overlook, but which it is incumbent to bear in mind, viz.:—That eager and enthusiastic disciples sometimes have visions and dream dreams, and that they are apt innocently to imagine or purposely to invent extraordinary or supernatural events worthy the imagined importance of the subject, and answering the burning zeal of their faith. The calm observer and sincere interpreter of nature cannot set capricious or arbitrary bounds to his inquiries at any point where another may assert that he ought to do so ; he cannot choose but claim and maintain the right to search and try what any man, Jew or Gentile, Mussulman or Brahmin, has declared sacred, and to see if it be true. And if it be not true to him, what matters it how true it be? The theologian tells him that the limits of philosophical inquiry are where faith begins, but he is concerned to find out where faith does begin, and to examine what sort of evidence the evidence of things unseen is. And if this right of free inquiry be denied him, then is denied him the right to doubt what any visionary or fanatic, or madman, or impostor, may choose to proclaim as a revelation from the spiritual world.

Towards the close of his lecture the Archbishop, breaking out into peroration, becomes violently contemptuous of the philosopher who, " with his sensations sorted and tied up and labelled to the utmost, might," he thinks, " chance to find himself the most odious and ridiculous being in all the multiform creation. A creature so glib, so wise, so full of discourse, sitting in the midst of creation with all its mystery and wonder, and persuading you that he is the master of its secrets, and that there is nothing but what he knows !" It is not very difficult to raise a laugh by drawing a caricature; but it was hardly, perhaps, worthy the lecturer, the subject, and the audience, to exhibit on such an occasion an archiepiscopal talent for drawing caricatures. As we have already intimated, this philosopher, " so glib, so wise, so full of discourse," does

not profess to know nearly so much of the mystery
and wonder of creation as the Archbishop does. There
is more flourishing language of the same sort before
the discourse ends, but it would be unprofitable to
transcribe or criticise it; and it is only right to the
lecturer to say that he is near his conclusion when he
works himself up into this vituperative and somewhat
hysterical ecstasy. The following passage may be
quoted, however, as instructive in more respects than
one :—

"The world offers just now the spectacle, humiliating to us in
many ways, of millions of people clinging to their old idolatrous
religions, and refusing to change them even for a higher form ; whilst
in Christian Europe thousands of the most cultivated class are beginning to consider atheism a permissible or even a desirable thing.
The very instincts of the savage rebuke us. But just when we seem
in danger of losing all may come the moment of awakening to the
dangers of our loss. A world where thought is a secretion of the
brain-gland,—where free will is the dream of a madman that thinks
he is an emperor, though naked and in chains,—where God is not
or at least not knowable, such is not the world as we have learnt it,
on which great lives have been lived out, great self-sacrifices dared,
great piety and devotion have been bent on softening the sin, the
ignorance, and the misery. It is a world from which the sun is
withdrawn, and with it all light and life. But this is not *our* world
as it was, not the world of our fathers. To live is to think and to
will. To think is to see the chain of facts in creation, and passing
along its golden links to find the hand of God at its beginning, as
we saw His handiwork in its course. And to will is to be able to
know good and evil ; and to will aright is to submit the will entirely
to a will higher than ours. So that with God alone can we find true
knowledge and true rest, the vaunted fruits of philosophy."

Was ever before such a terrible indictment against
Christianity drawn by a Christian prelate ? Its doctrines

have now been preached for nearly two thousand years ; they have had the aids of vast armies, of incalculable wealth, of the greatest genius and eloquence ; they are embodied in the results of conquests, in the sublimest works of art, in some of the noblest specimens of oratory, in the very organization of modern society ; thousands upon thousands have died martyrs to their faith in them, and thousands more have been made martyrs for want of faith in them ; they have been carried to the darkest places of the earth by the vehicles of commerce, have been proclaimed by the messengers and backed by the moral power of a higher civilization ; they are almost identified with the spirit and results of modern scientific progress : all these advantages they have had, and yet the Archbishop can do no more than point to the spectacle of millions of people clinging to their old idolatrous religions, and to thousands of the most cultivated class in Christian Europe who are beginning to consider atheism a permissible or even a desirable thing ! Whether it be really true that so many of the cultivated class in Europe are gravitating towards atheism we cannot say ; but if the allegation be true, it may well be doubted whether an appeal to the instincts of the savage who persists in clinging to his idolatry will avail to convince them of their error. It is not very consistent on the Archbishop's part to make such an appeal, who in another paragraph of his lecture emphatically enjoins on philosophy not to banish God, freedom, duty, and immortality from the field of its inquiries, adjuring it solemnly never to consent to abandon these highest subjects of study.

Another comment on the passage above quoted which suggests itself is that men have undergone great self-sacrifices, sufferings, and death for a bad cause with as firm and cheerful a resolution as good men have for the best cause; to die for a faith is no proof whatever of the truth of it, nor by any means always the best service which a man may render it. Atheism counts its martyrs as well as Christianity. Jordano Bruno, the friend of Sir Philip Sidney, was condemned for atheism, sentenced to death, and, refusing to recant, burnt at the stake. Vanini, who suffered death as an atheist, might have been pardoned the moment before his execution if he would have retracted his doctrines; but he chose to be burnt to ashes rather than retract. To these might be added others who have gone through much persecution and grievous suffering for a cause which the Archbishop of York would count the worst for which a man could suffer. How many Christians of one sect have undergone lingering tortures and cruel deaths at the hands of Christians of another sect for the sake of small and non-essential points of doctrine in which only they differed—for points at issue so minute as to " be scarcely visible to the nicest theological eye !" Christianity has sometimes been a terrible war-cry, and it must be confessed that Christians have been good persecutors. When the passions of men have worked a faith into enthusiasm, they will suffer and die, and inflict suffering and death, for any cause, good or bad.

The appeal to the martyrdom of professors is therefore of small worth as an argument for the truth of their doctrine. Pity 'tis that it is so, for if it were otherwise, if self-sacrifice in a cause would suffice to establish it, what a noble and powerful argument in support of the Christian verities might archbishops and bishops offer, in these sad times of luxury and unbelief when so many are lapsing into atheism?

But we must bring to an end these reflections, which are some of those that have been suggested by the perusal of the archiepiscopal address on the Limits of Philosophical Inquiry. Though heavy charges are laid against modern science, they are made in a thoughtless rather than a bitter spirit, while the absence of bigotry and the general candour displayed may justify a hope that the author will, on reflection, perceive his opinions to require further consideration, and his statements to be too indiscriminate and sweeping. On the whole there is, we think, less reason to apprehend harm to scientific inquiry from this discharge of the Archbishop's feelings, than to apprehend harm to those who are obstinately defending the religious position against the attack which is thought imminent. For he has used his friends badly: he has exposed their entire flank to the enemy; while he would distinctly have philosophy concern itself with the highest subjects—God, freedom, and immortality—despising a philosophy which forbears to do so, and pointing out how miserably it falls short of its highest mission, he warns philosophy in the same breath that there is a point at which its teaching ends.

"Philosophy, whilst she is teaching morals and religion, will soon come to a point where her teaching tends . . . She will send her scholars to seek in revelation and practical obedience the higher culture that she can only commence."

The pity of the matter is, that we are not furnished with a word of guidance as to where the hitherto and no farther point is. With brave and flourishing words he launches the inquirer on a wide waste of waters, but without a rudder to guide him, or a compass to steer by. Is he to go on so long as what he discovers is in conformity with the Gospel according to the Thirty-nine Articles, but furl to his sails, cease his exertions, and go down on his knees the moment his discoveries clash with the faith according to the Thirty-nine Articles? What guarantee have we that he will be content to do so? In withholding the Scriptures from the people, and shutting off philosophy entirely from the things that belong to faith, the Church of Rome occupies a strong and almost impregnable position; for if there be no reading there will be no inquiry, and if there be no inquiry there will be no doubt, and if there be no doubt there will be no disbelief. But the union of philosophical inquiry and religious faith is not a natural union of kinds; and it is difficult to see how the product of it can be much different from the hybrid products of other unnatural unions of different kinds—can be other than sterile, when it is not monstrous.

THE THEORY OF VITALITY.[1]

It has been the custom of certain disciples of the so-called Positive Philosophy to repudiate as extravagant the well-known opinion of Protagoras, that man was the measure of the universe. If the proposition be understood of man as he is known to himself by the revelations of self-consciousness, there is unquestionably great reason for its rejection ; but if it be applied to him as an objective study, it is manifest that modern science is tending to prove it by no means so absurd as it has been sometimes deemed. Day by day, indeed, is it becoming more and more clear that, as Sir T. Browne has it, man "parallels nature in the cosmography of himself;" that, in truth, "we are that bold and adventurous piece of nature which he that studies wisely learns in a compendium what others labour at in a divided piece and endless volume." [2] The "heaven-descended γνῶθι σεαυτόν" acquires new value as a maxim inculcating on man the objective study of himself.

[1] British and Foreign Medico-Chir. Review, No. 64. 1863.
[2] Religio Medici.

The earliest cultivators of Grecian philosophy—Thales, Anaximenes, and Diogenes of Apollonia—did seek objectively for the ἀρχή or first principle of things common to man and the rest of nature.   This primitive kind of induction was soon, however, abandoned for the easier and speedier deduction from the subjective facts of consciousness ; so that, as the German philosopher is said to have done with the elephant, man constructed the laws of an external world out of the depths of his own consciousness.   Because an individual was conscious of certain passions which influenced his conduct, he fancied that natural bodies were affected in their relations to one another by like passions.   Hence the phenomena of nature were explained by sympathies, antipathies, loves, discords : oil had an antipathy to water ; nature abhorred a vacuum ; Love was the creative force which produced development and harmony ; Hate, the destructive force which produced disorder and discord.   The method was only a phase of the anthropomorphism by which the Dryad was placed in the tree, the Naiad in the fountain, and the gods of mankind were created by man.

The result of such a method was inevitable.   When in a language there is but one word for two or three different meanings, as happens in all languages before the cultivation of science—when, for example, the loadstone is said to attract iron, the earth to attract heavy bodies, the plant to attract moisture, and one mind to attract another, without further differentiation—there necessarily is an ambiguity about words ; disputes thereupon arise, and the unavoidable issue is sophistry and sophists.   That

was a result which the ingenious and active mind of
Greece soon reached. In scientific nomenclature it is
constantly becoming necessary to discard words which
are in common use, because of their vagueness and want
of precision ; for as it is with life objectively, and as it is
with cognition or life subjectively, so must it be with the
language in which the phenomena are expressed. A scientific nomenclature must rightly present a progress from
the general to the special, must reflect in its increasing
specialization the increased specialization of human
adaptation to external nature. As might be expected,
Plato and Aristotle both recognized the evil in Greece,
and both tried to check it. The metaphysics, analytics,
&c. of the latter have been described as a dictionary
of general terms, "the process throughout being first to
discover and establish definite meanings, and then to appropriate to each a several word."[1] But it is in vain to
attempt to establish words except as living outgrowths of
actual facts in nature. The method was a mistaken one ;
there was not an intending of the mind to the realities of
external nature, and knowledge was barren, wanting those
"fruits and invented works" which Bacon pronounces to

[1] Coleridge's Literary Correspondence. It is for this attempt,
praiseworthy surely as far as it went, that Bacon is unduly severe
upon Aristotle in some parts. Thus : "And herein I cannot a little
marvel at the philosopher Aristotle that did proceed in such a spirit
of difference and contradiction towards all antiquity, undertaking
not only to form new words of science at pleasure, but to confound
and extinguish all ancient wisdom." (De Augmentis Scientiarum.)
And again : "Aristotle, as though he had been of the race of the
Ottomans, thought he could not reign except the first thing he did he
killed all his brethren." (Ibid.)

L

be, as it were, "sponsors and sureties for the truth of philosophy."

Much the same thing happened in the earlier part of the Middle Ages. The mysticism and sophistry which then prevailed, the endless and unprofitable but learned and ingenious disputes concerning empty propositions and words which had no definite meanings, might be said to represent the wasted efforts and unavailing strength of a blind giant. But as the infant, moved by an internal impulse, at first strives unconsciously for its mother's breast and draws its nourishment therefrom, gradually awakening thereby to a consciousness of the mother who supplies it, so the human mind for a time gathered unconsciously the material of its knowledge from nature, until it was gradually awakened to a full consciousness of the fruitful bosom which was supplying it. The alchemist, moved by his avarice and the instinct of a unity in nature, and the astrologer, moved by the feeling of a destiny governing human actions, both lighted on treasures which, though not then appreciated, were yet not lost; for of astrology came astronomy, and from alchemy, in the fulness of time, was born chemistry. In Roger Bacon, who successfully interrogated nature in the spirit of the inductive method, we see the human·mind instinctively and, as it were, unconsciously striving after the true source of knowledge; while in the Chancellor Bacon, who established the principles and systematized the rules of the inductive philosophy, we see it awakened to a clear apprehension of the necessity of doing with design and method that which in an imperfect manner it had for some time been blindly aiming at. But as it is with the infant, so it was with humanity : action preceded consciousness, and Bacon was the efflux of a spirit which prevailed, and not the creator of it.

The method of investigation has accordingly been completely reversed. Instead of beginning with himself and passing thence to external nature, man begins with nature and ends with himself ; he is the complex to which his investigations ascend step by step through progressively increasing complications of the simple. Not only so, but the necessity of studying himself objectively is fully recognized ; it is not the subjective feeling of heat or cold in a feverish patient, but the figure at which the thermometer stands, that is now appealed to as the trustworthy index of the real temperature. The development of the senses, or, in other words, the increased specialty of human adaptation to external nature, has been, as the progress of science proves, the foundation of intellectual advance; the understanding has been developed through the senses, and has in turn constructed instruments for extending the action of the senses.[1] The telescope has merely been a means for enabling the eye to penetrate into distant space, and to observe the

---

[1] A great desideratum is a history of such development of the senses : " Wir besitzen gar treffliche Werke über die Geschichte von Schlachten und Staatsformen, genaue Tagebücher von Königen und fleissige Verzeichnisse von den Schöpfungen der Dichter. Aber den wichtigsten Beitrag zu einer Bildungsgeschichte des Menschen in der eingreifendsten Bedeutung des Wortes hat noch Niemand geliefert. Uns fehlt eine Entwickelungsgeschichte der Sinne."—MOLESCHOTT, *Kreislauf des Lebens.*

motions of worlds which the unaided vision would never
have revealed ; by the microscope the minute structure
of tissues and the history of the little world of the
organic cell has been made known ; the balance has de-
monstrated the indestructibility of matter, and has supplied to science the exactness of the numerical method ;
and, in the electric stream, there has been found a means
of investigating nerve action, like that which there is in
polarized light for ascertaining the internal condition of
crystallized bodies.   Who would have ventured to predict some time since that it would ever be possible to
measure the speed at which an impulse of the will travels
along the nerves ?[1]   And who will venture to say that it
will not at a future time be possible to measure the velo-

---

[1] Such an eminent physiologist as Müller could venture to predict
the impossibility thereof. In his Physiology he says : "Wir werden
auch wohl nie die Mittel gewinnen die Geschwindigkeit der Nerven-
wirkung zu ermitteln da uns die Vergleich. ungeheurer Entfernung
felht aus der die Schnelligkeit einer dem Nerven in dieser Hinsicht
analogen Wirkung des Licht berechnet werden kann."   With which
compare Helmholtz : " Ueber die Methoden kleinste Zeittheilchen
zu messen," &c.   1850.

" As long as physiologists considered it necessary to refer the operations of the nerves to the extension of an imponderable or psychical
principle, it might well appear incredible that the rapidity of the
stream should be measurable within the limits of the animal body.
At present we know, from the investigations of Du Bois-Reymond
on the electro-motor properties of nerves, that the activity by which
the propagation of a stimulus is accomplished is closely connected
with an altered arrangement of their material molecules—perhaps
even essentially determined by them.   Accordingly, the process of
conduction in nerves may belong to the series of continuous molecular operations of ponderable bodies, in which, for example, the
conduction of sound in the air, or the combustion in a tube filled

city with which one idea calls up another in the brain ? Biology must plainly of necessity be the last and most difficult study, for it presupposes the other sciences as vital force supposes inferior forces ; but it is the evident tendency of advancing knowledge to bring life more and more within the compass of scientific investigation. And if it be sometimes made a reproach to science, as it was by Comte, that it has not discovered the laws of life, it may well rest calm under the censure, pointing to the history of the earth to show that nature, having done all else, required a long period before it accomplished the evolution of life.

In spite, then, of a desire on the part of some persons to separate biology from the other sciences, and notwithstanding the alarm occasionally displayed with regard to the dignity of vitality, it is the certain tendency of advancing knowledge to bring a science of life into close and indissoluble relations with other sciences, and thus to establish in cognition, or to reflect in consciousness, the unity which exists in nature. When, in ancient times, life was assigned to the stars, the air, the water, a sort of unity was recognized, but recognized only by explaining nature from a very imperfect knowledge of man ; now the task is to explain man on the basis of an increasing knowledge of nature, and in that way to demonstrate the unity of the whole. What must be the result ? Nothing less, indeed, than the reconciliation of the ideal and the

with an explosive mixture, is to be reckoned.   It is not surprising, therefore," he adds, "that the speed of conduction should be very moderate." (Ueber die Methoden, &c.)

real, the identification of subjective and objective. As
life is a condition in which an intimate correlation exists
between the individual and nature, it is evident that whilst
Plato dealt only with *ideas* of the mind, his system must
remain comparatively unprofitable ; but it is evident also
that since we have learnt to discover the *laws* or *ideas*
in nature of which *ideas* in the mind are correlates, it
becomes possible to find in nature an interpretation of
Plato's true ideas.[1] Once for all, it may perhaps be taken
for granted that the ideas of genius never can be meaningless ; for its mental life is a reflection in consciousness
of the unconscious life of nature. How excellently has
this been exemplified in him who embodied in poetical
form the scientific spirit of this age ! It was the great
characteristic of Goethe, as Lavater justly said of him, to
give a poetical form to the real ; he proved, in fact, that
science, in place of rendering poetry impossible, opened
a field for the highest poetry. His romance of the
Elective Affinities (*Wahlverswandschaften*) starts from the
chemical affinities of elements, and applies such affinities
to human beings, therein exactly reversing the old method
which, starting from the phenomena of self-consciousness,
applied the passions of the human mind to the phenomena of external nature. Of Goethe it may be justly

[1] " But it is manifest that Plato, in his opinion of ideas as one
that had a wit of elevation situate as upon a cliff, did descry
' that forms were the true object of knowledge,' but lost the real
fruit of his opinion by considering of forms as absolutely abstracted
from matter, and not confined and determined by matter ; and so
turning his opinion on theology, wherewith all his natural philosophy
is infected."—*De Aug. Scient.*

said, that in him the ideal and the real were happily
blended ; that he embodied the scientific spirit of the
age, and yet was in some respects an advance upon it ;
that he was a prophecy of that which must be a course
of development of the human mind if it be destined
to develop.

The foregoing general sketch of the course and tendency of knowledge is fully justified by the present aspect
of science. When nature was first examined objectively
the differences in matter appeared manifold, and its modes
of energy or activity—that is, its forces—appeared many
also. On a more careful use of the senses, however,—
in fact, by the application of the delicate balance to the
products of combustion,—it became evident that one
form of matter only disappeared to reappear in another
form ; that it never perished, but only changed. Elementary matter thus passes upwards into chemical and
organic compounds, and then downwards from organic to
chemical, and from chemical compounds to its elementary
condition. Out of dust man is formed by an upward
transformation of matter, and to dust he returns by a
retrograde metamorphosis thereof. Corresponding with
the changes in the form of matter are changes in its
modes of energy or its forces ; to different combinations
and arrangements of molecules correspond different
modes of energy. Force therefore is eternal, like matter,
and passes through a corresponding cycle of transformations. The correlation and conservation of forces, which
have always been more or less clearly recognized as
necessities of human thought, are now accepted as

scientific axioms, and are daily receiving experimental demonstration.[1]

Though it may seem difficult to avoid the conclusion that there is fundamentally but one natural force which manifests itself under different modes, yet such a supposition at present transcends the domain of science. As a matter of fact we are compelled, in order to form a satisfactory conception of matter and its forces, to regard it under a twofold aspect. In all our conceptions we imply a sort of dualism of power in every body, though we are very apt to forget it in our generalizations. The hinges of gravitation, for example, keep worlds in their orbits by opposing a centrifugal force which would otherwise drive them afloat into space. The smaller hinges of molecular cohesion hold together the infinitely smaller bodies which we call molecules of matter, in opposition to a repulsive force, which, on the application of a little heat, may drive them off into space, and in volatile substances does so drive them off without heat. It is the same with liquids; their diffusion power is similar in character to the volatility of solids; while

---

[1] Epicurus, Democritus, Aristotle, all upheld the eternity of matter; the quotations from Lucretius and Persius on that subject are well known, but the following passage from the *De Augmentis* is not so common : " All things change, but nothing is lost. This is an axiom in physics, and holds in natural theology; for as the sum of matter neither diminishes nor increases, so it is equally the work of Omnipotence to create or to annihilate." Other passages of like import occur in Bacon's writings. And the Brahminical doctrine is as follows : "The ignorant assert that the universe in the beginning did not exist in its author, and that it was created out of nothing. O ye, whose hearts are pure, how could something come out of nothing ? "

"colloids" are volatile, "crystalloids" are comparatively "fixed." There is a relation of molecules to one another which we are compelled to represent in conception as the result of a force of repulsion or tension. And as some sensible image is necessary for the mind in order to the clearness of a conception of the invisible, physics assumes between the ponderable molecules of a body certain ethereal particles which are in a state of stationary oscillation, the degree of temperature of the body being supposed to depend upon the intensity of the active force of these imponderable intermolecular particles. If the body be suddenly and greatly compressed, these motions are communicated to the imponderable ether outside the body, and tension force thus becomes free force in manifest radiation of heat. "What is heat in us," very justly said Locke, "is in the heated body nothing but motion." When heat is withdrawn from matter—that is, when the tension force becomes free, its molecules get nearer to one another—their cohesion is greater; thus vapours become liquids and liquids become solids.

It seems probable that the necessity of regarding matter under this twofold aspect of attraction and repulsion is owing to man's inability, as being himself a part of nature, to form a conception of nature as a whole. He must necessarily regard things in relation to himself; for as he exists only in relation to nature, and as every phase of consciousness is an expression of this relation, it is plain that one of the elements of the relation cannot free itself, and from an independent point of view watch unconcernedly things as they really are. Thus, though we speak of passivity and activity, they are really not different kinds of action, but different relations of the same kind of action. Whatever be the cause, and however doubtful the philosophical validity of the distinction, we are compelled to regard matter in this two-fold relation. One aspect of the relation we describe as passive, statical, cohesion, or, to use the generic term, attraction; the other is active, dynamical, tension, or, to use the generic term, repulsion. Attraction plus repulsion of molecules constitutes our conception of matter; and in observation of its modes of energy, attraction is recognized in gravitation, cohesion, magnetism, affinity, love, while repulsion is found in the centrifugal force, in heat, in electricity, in antipathy and hate.

It is in rising to the department of chemical compounds that attraction is found under a new and special phase as chemical affinity. But when the chemical union of two molecules into a single one takes place, a diminution of the tension force surrounding each molecule must occur, and, according to the law of the conservation of force, an equivalent of another force must be set free. This happens in the production of heat and electricity; for, as Faraday has shown, chemical action cannot take place without the development of electricity. The amount of force liberated in a simple chemical combination will be the equivalent of the tension force lost. When one atom of carbon combines with one atom of oxygen, a definite quantity of tension force surrounding each molecule disappears, and a definite quantity of heat is accordingly produced. When two molecules separate in chemical decomposition, they necessarily make passive or latent so much active force; so much heat becomes so much tension force. But furthermore, in a chemical decomposition we have the resolution of that very intense and special force, chemical affinity itself; so that the force set free will, one would suppose, far exceed that which becomes latent as tension force around the molecules. We know not why two molecules should chemically combine; we accept as a fundamental law of their nature this high, special, and powerful form of attraction; but we do know that when chemical decomposition takes place a little chemical force must be resolved into a large display of inferior force. It is a fact authenticated by Faraday, that one drop of water contains, and may be made to evolve, as much electricity as under different modes of display would suffice to produce a lightning flash. The decomposition of matter is the resolution of force, and in such resolution one equivalent of chemical force will correspond to several equivalents of inferior force. Thus chemical force, though correlated with the physical forces, may be said to be of a much higher order than they are.

In the still higher stage of matter in a state of vitality, we meet with chemical combination of a much more complex character than occurs in inorganic matter; attraction appears under its most special and complex form. Matter, which in its elementary condition might occupy some space, is so blended or combined as to occupy a minimum of space; and force which, under

a lower mode, might suffice perhaps to illuminate the
heavens, is here confined within the small compass of
an organic cell or of a speck of protoplasm. We have
to do, however, with organic matter under two forms—
as dead and as living matter, as displaying energy of its
own, or as displaying no energy.   Dead organic matter
has ceased to act, and it is now acted upon ; it is at the
mercy of the forces which surround it, and immediately
begin to effect its dissolution.   Heat hastens decomposition, because in the separation of the constituents of
organic matter into the ultimate inorganic products,—carbonic acid, ammonia, and water,—a certain amount of
active force must become latent as the tension force of
these molecules ; and this force the heat supplies.   There
is also the force of the chemical affinity of the oxygen of
the air for the oxidizable elements of the substance ; and
the combination is necessarily attended with the production of heat.   The heating value of organic matter will
accordingly increase with the quantity of oxidizable elements ; but the matter is by no means so simple as it
might at first sight appear to be.   Suppose the atom of
carbon with which an atom of oxygen combines was
previously in combination with, for example, an atom of
hydrogen ; and the question is, whether the amount of
heat produced will be the same as though the atom of
carbon had been free ?   In reality it will not ; it must be
less, because in the separation of the carbon atom and
the hydrogen atom so much active force must become
tension force—that is, so much heat must disappear or
become latent ; and that loss of heat will necessarily

counterbalance a part of the heat produced, or the decrease of tension force 'which occurs, through the combination of the atom of carbon with the atom of oxygen. It is this consideration which appears to invalidate some experiments made and conclusions come to with regard to animal heat.

But there is another consideration. In this mere burning or decomposition of organic matter, or that which represents the passive, statical, or attractive phase of vitality, the active.force which results is due partly to force from without, and not solely to the liberation of force latent in the matter. External forces have, as it were, been pulling it to pieces. What, then, on the principle of the conservation of force, becomes of that intense chemical force which is implied in the organic nature of the material, that power which holds it together as a specific material differing in properties from all kinds of inorganic matter? Though dead, the chemical composition of organic substance is the same as when alive; and its future destiny is entirely dependent on the circumstances in which it may be placed. In the air, it is true, it will undergo decomposition into inorganic products; but if it be surrounded with the conditions of life, if it be exposed to the influence of higher forces by being given as food to some animal, it does not go downwards, but upwards, and somehow takes on life again. It is plain what becomes of the statical force under the latter circumstances. But in the decomposition of organic matter in the air and the correlative resolution of force, it is not so evident what

becomes of all the force which must be liberated.
That it returns to general nature can admit of no
doubt; but does it all appear as heat? A part of it
must necessarily do so, becoming latent as the tension
force of the molecules of the ultimate products of its
decomposition, and the rest is liberated under some
form or other, if not entirely as heat. There is some
reason to believe, however, that dead organic substance
does not always undergo the extreme retrograde metamorphosis of material and of force before being used
up again in vital compounds, even by the vegetable
kingdom. It has been shown that not only do pale
plants, such as fungi, feed on organic matter, but that
soluble humus is regularly taken up by the roots of
almost all plants. Professor Le Conte has shown it
to be probable that the decomposition of the organic
matter supplies the force necessary for raising other
matter from a lower to a higher stage.[1] The force
necessary for organization is thus furnished by the force
which results from disorganization; death and destruction are the conditions of life and development.

When organic matter displays energy—that is, when it
has life—its relations with its surroundings are different.
As chemical affinity seems to hold the place of attraction in it, and to correspond to gravitation amongst
celestial bodies, cohesive force amongst molecules, and

[1] The Correlation of Physical, Chemical, and Vital Force, and
the Conservation of Force in Vital Phenomena. By J. Le Conte,
Professor of Geology and Chemistry in South Carolina College.
(American Journal of Science and Arts, No. 28, 1859.)

magnetic force amongst polar molecules, so its dynamical or vital action seems to correspond to the force of repulsion, to the centrifugal force of heavenly bodies, the tension force of molecules, and electrical repulsion. The display of energy coincides with a molecular change in the statical element. With the function of a ganglionic nerve-cell, for example, a correlative molecular change, or "waste," as it is called, necessarily takes place either in the nerve element itself or in what is supplied to it from the blood. The substances which are met with in the so-called extractives of nerve-tissue afford abundant evidence of a material waste; for as products of the retrograde metamorphosis are found lactic acid in considerable quantities, kreatin, uric acid, probably also hypoxanthin, and representing the fatty acids, formic and acetic acid.[1] And what Du Bois-Reymond proved to happen in muscle, Funke has observed to happen also with nerve : while the contents of nerve-tubes are neutral during rest in the living state, they become acid after death, and also after great activity during life. After excessive mental exercise, it is well known that phosphates appear in the urine in considerable quantities; and it is only by supposing an idea to be accompanied by a correlative change in the nerve-cells that we can explain the bodily exhaustion which is produced by mental labour, and the breaking

[1] It is interesting to remark how the products of chemical transformation resulting from nerve action agree with the products of decomposition after muscular activity, and how the results coincide with what, *a priori*, might have been expected from the great vital activity of nerve-structure.

down of the brain under prolonged intellectual efforts.
There is even at times a sensation of something going
on in the brain ; and in insanity, such anomalous
feelings are sometimes persistently complained of. But
the change or waste which accompanies energy is re-
stored by nutrition during rest, and the conditions of
future energy are thus established ; nutritive attraction
steadily reparing the waste of centrifugal function. The
cell thus, for a time at least, preserves its individuality ;
and definiteness of energy, with the maintenance of
individuality, are what is connoted by vitality.

Is the energy displayed by living matter something,
quite special? In attempting to answer that question
two considerations should be kept in view. In the first
place, an effect need not at all resemble in properties its
cause ; the qualities of a chemical compound are quite
different from those of its constituents. Such a complex
compound as organic matter really is may be expected,
therefore, to exhibit peculiar properties in no way resembling those of its constituent elements or those of simple
compounds. In the second place, the arrangement or
grouping of the molecules in a substance, independently
of its chemical composition, may greatly alter its properties : there is a molecular as well as a chemical constitution of matter. In that condition of bodies which is
described as Isomerism, there are atoms alike in number,
nature, and relative proportion, so grouped as somehow
to produce compounds having very different chemical
properties. Again, it has been found that the same
matter may exist under two very different conditions,

and with very different properties,—as colloidal and as crystalloidal, in a gelatinous or in a crystalline state. And what is the chief difference? It is that the colloidal is a dynamical state of matter, the crystalloidal a statical state. The colloid exhibits energy; its existence is a continued metastasis; and it may be looked upon, says Graham, "as the probable primary source of the force appearing in the phenomena of vitality." The distinction between the two kinds of matter is, in fact, "that subsisting between the material of a mineral and the material of an organized mass." And yet minerals may exist in the colloidal state; the hydrated peroxides of the aluminous class, for example, are colloids. Furthermore, the mineral forms of silicic acid deposited from water, such as flint, are found to have passed during the geological ages from the colloidal into the crystalline condition; and, on the other hand, in the so-called blood-crystals of Funke, a soft and gelatinous albuminoid is seen to assume a crystalline contour. "Can any facts," asks Graham, "more strikingly illustrate the maxim, that in nature there are no abrupt transitions, and that distinctions of class are never absolute?"[1]

[1] A further characteristic of colloids is their singular inertness in all ordinary chemical relations, though they have a compensating activity of their own in their penetrability; they are permeable when in mass, as water is, by the more highly diffusive class of substances, but they cut off entirely other colloidal substances that may be in solution. It is evident that our conception of solid matter must soon undergo considerable modification. (On Liquid Diffusion applied to Analysis. By T. Graham, F.R.S. Philosophical Transactions, 1862.)

M

The foregoing considerations render it evident that the manifestation of organic energy by matter is not a contrast to the kind of energy which is displayed by inorganic matter, and so far justify the supposition that it may be a question of chemical composition and intimate molecular constitution.   Vitality would not then be a special principle, but a result, and would be explained ultimately by the operation of the so-called molecular forces.   Coleridge's assertion, that the division of substances into living and dead, though *psychologically* necessary, was of doubtful philosophical validity, would receive a support which its author could scarce have expected for it.

Before granting any conclusion, it is desirable to examine into that which is generally deemed to constitute the specialty of life.   Now it is certain, when we consider the vast range of vitality from the simple life of a molecule or cell to the complex life of man, that valid objections may be made to any definition of life.   If it be wide enough to comprise all forms, it will be too vague to have any value; if narrow enough to be exact, it will exclude the most lowly forms.   The problem is to investigate the conditions of the manifestation of life.   A great fault in many attempted definitions has been the description of life as a resistance or complete contrast to the rest of nature, which was supposed to be continually striving to destroy it.   But the elements of organic matter are not different from those of inorganic, whence they are derived, and to which they return; and the chemical and mechanical forces of these elements cannot be suspended or removed within the organism. What is special is the manner of composition of the elements : there is a concurrence of manifold substances, and they are combined or grouped together in a very complex way. Such union or grouping is, however, only a further advance upon, and by no means a contrast to, the kind of combination which is met with in inorganic bodies. Life is not a contrast to non-living nature, but a further development of it. The more knowledge advances, the more plainly is it shown that there are physical and chemical processes upon which life depends. Heat is produced by combustion in the organism as it is in the fire ; starch is converted into sugar there, as it is in the chemical laboratory ; urea, which is so constant a product of the body's chemistry, can be formed artificially by the chemist ; and the process of excitation in a nerve, on the closure of a constant stream, appears to be analogous to the process of electrolysis in which hydrogen is given off at the negative pole.[1] The peculiarity of life is the complexity of combination in so small a space, the intimate operation of many simultaneously acting forces in the microcosm of the organic cell. Knowledge cannot pass the life-boundary, because there are not at present any means of following the intimate changes which take place beyond it ; there is a world there into which the senses of man cannot yet enter. But as each great advance of science has followed some invention by which the operation of the senses has been extended,

[1] A. von Bezold : Untersuchungen über die electrische Erregung der Nerven und Muskeln. Leipzig, 1861.

there can be little doubt that the important step towards
a true science of life will be made with the discovery of
a means of tracing the delicate processes of protoplasmic
activity. Microscopic physics and microscopic chemistry,
nay physics and chemistry of a delicacy beyond the reach
of the powers of the highest microscope, are needed. So
that it may well be that this generation and generations
to come will have passed to their everlasting rest before
a discovery of the secret of vital activity is made.

Before dealing with that which is considered to mark
a second and great peculiarity of life, namely, its aim or
plan, it will be well to illustrate the foregoing remarks
from the phenomena of conscious vitality. It is, in
truth, with the lowest form of vitality as it is with the
lowest form of conscious vitality—with the human mind
in the earliest stages of its evolution. A self-conser-
vative impulse moves the most barbarous people to
regard the operation of the external forces of nature, and
to adopt rude means to preserve life and to obtain comfort; the savage avoids the current which would drive
his frail canoe on the hungry breakers, and shelters his
hut from the overwhelming fury of the storm ; he may
be said to war with nature for the maintenance of individual power, as the vital force of a cell may be said to
war with the nature that immediately surrounds it. But
it is obvious that man only struggles successfully with
the physical forces by recognizing the laws of their
action, and by accommodating his individual forces to
physical laws ; it is victory by obedience. By conscious
obedience to the physical law, he appropriates, as it

were, the force thereof, in the increase of his own power ;
the idea is developed in his mind as the correlate of the
law or idea in nature ; in his mental progress nature is
undergoing development through him. By keeping in
mind this analogy of the mental force the difficulty will
be obviated, which there might seem to be in conceiving
the organic cell as a result of physical and chemical
forces, and yet as resisting the action of these forces.
Every act of so-called resistance on the part of the cell
to the natural forces is really a phenomenon indicating
the development of them ; its life is not a contrast to
non-living nature, but a further complication of it. The
fundamental law of life is the same for its conscious and
unconscious manifestations ; it is individuation by appro-
priation. And however necessary it may seem to the
individual, as a part of a whole looking at the rest, to
represent the vital as in constant antagonism to the
physical, such a conception does not faithfully express
the condition of the whole regarded as a whole. A just
conception of nature as one harmonious whole is plainly
not antagonistic to the spirit of any investigations which
may tend to prove the dependence of life on physical
and chemical processes.

That which is commonly said to constitute the
specialty of life is the maintenance of a certain definite
plan ; and accordingly Coleridge, following Schelling,
defined life as "the principle of individuation." Given
the different kinds of force and of matter, and how, it is
asked, is the pattern determined and worked out ? As
every individual is in life weaving out some pattern " on

the roaring loom of time," though "what he weaves no weaver knows," so the lowest form of vitality manifests a definite energy, and is said to accomplish a definite plan. A crystal would go on increasing if suitable materials and the conditions of its growth were present, "but it has been provided that trees do not grow up into heaven." Life works according to an aim, said Aristotle. Admitting all this, we are not therefore called upon to admit a special contrast to the rest of nature. Liebig compares the living body to a building which is constructed after a definite, pre-ordained plan; but it is obvious that exactly in the same sense might the positive biologist say of the chemical atom, that it is constructed and displays energy according to a pre-ordained plan; or even of the crystal, that it works out a certain pattern, seeing that it cannot overstep the laws of its form. The plan is the law of the matter; and the law is not something outside the matter, but it is inherent in it. Organic matter, like the chemical element, has an activity given to itself which it must display; the law of causality is true of it as of inorganic matter; and the organic effect, the so-called accomplishment of the plan, is the necessary result of a certain molecular constitution and certain intimate combinations which exist in the organic molecule or cell or monad, or whatever else we choose to name the ultimate unit of life.

The direct denial of a special vital force has been the natural reaction against that dogmatism which assumed a vital principle that was self-generating, did anything it liked, and was not amenable to investigation. That any force should be self-generating in inexhaustible quantity is really an inconceivable supposition. If the axiom that force, like matter, is not capable of annihilation, be accepted, and we find, as we do, that organic bodies incorporate, or somehow cause to disappear, inorganic matter and force, and thereby themselves increase, it is an unavoidable conclusion that the organic matter and force must represent the converted inorganic matter and force. To suppose that the vital force was self-produced would be to suppose a disturbance of the equilibrium of nature, and it might not then be unreasonable to fear lest the earth, by the increase of its repulsion force, should break through the hinges of gravitation and float off into space, or burst into fragments, as a planet between Mars and Jupiter is supposed at one time to have done.[1]

When, however, it is said that a minute portion of living matter converts inorganic matter into its own nature, and thus develops new organic matter which

[1] Science, in its view of life, seems to be following the course of development in Humboldt's mind. In his earlier writings he defined vital force as the unknown cause which prevents the elements from following their original attractive forces. (Aphorism. ex doct. Phys. Chem. Plant.) "Reflection and prolonged study," he says, in his 'Aspects of Nature,' "in the departments of physiology and chemistry, have deeply shaken my earlier belief in peculiar so-called vital force." And again : "The difficulty of satisfactorily referring the vital phenomena of organism to physical and chemical laws depends chiefly (and almost in the same manner as the prediction of meteorological processes in the atmosphere) on the complication of the phenomena, and on the great number of the simultaneously-acting forces, as well as the conditions of their activity."

has the power of doing likewise, it is evident that a great and peculiar potentiality is assumed in the living molecule. What power is it which transforms the matter and force? Some who have advocated the correlation of the vital force with the physical forces seem not to have given due attention to this question: they have laid such great stress on the external force as to have fallen into an error almost as great as, though the opposite of, that of the advocates of a self-generating vital force. External circumstances are the necessary conditions of inward activity, but the inward fact is the important condition—it is the determining condition, and, so far as we know yet, it can only be derived from a like living mother structure. Nevertheless, even in that inherited potentiality there is not a contrast to that which happens in the rest of nature. When heat is converted into electricity, or any force into another, the change is not self-determined ; the determining force lies in the molecules of the matter, in the so-called statical force, that which Aristotle in his division of causes names the material cause. And if it be objected that a little life is able to do such a great deal, the answer is that a like thing happens in fermentation. When a certain organic substance makes the inorganic matter in contact with it become organic, it may be that it does so by a kind of infection or fermentation by which the molecular relations of its smallest particles are transferred to the particles of the inorganic, just as in the inorganic world forces pass from matter to matter.

But there are further considerations. Admitting that

the vital transforming matter is at first derived from vital structure, it is evident that the external force and matter transformed does in turn become transforming force— that is, vital. And if that takes place after the vital process *has once commenced*, is it, it may be asked, extravagant to suppose that a similar transformation might at some period have *commenced* the process, and may even now be doing so? The fact that in growth and development life is continually increasing from a transformation of physical and chemical forces, is after all in favour of the presumption that it may at first have so originated. And the advocate of this view may turn upon his opponent, and demand of him how he, with a due regard to the axiom that force is not self-generating, and to the fact that living matter does increase from the size of a little cell to the magnitude of a human body, accounts for the continual production of transforming power? A definite quantity only could have been derived from the mother structure, and that must have been exhausted at an early period of growth. The obvious refuge of the vitalist is to the facts that it is impossible now to evolve life artificially out of any combination of physical and chemical forces, and that such a transformation is never witnessed save under the conditions of vitality.

Thus the argument stands. Meanwhile, those who do believe in the origination of life from non-living matter hope to succeed in artificially producing the upward transformation, and may say reasonably enough that it is not to be expected that such transformation should now take place as a regular process in nature, except under conditions of vitality. Such a supposition is as unnecessary as it would be to assume that the savage must continue to rub together his sticks, after he has obtained the spark, in order to make the fire burn. What only is necessary is that the spark of fire, or the spark of life, once evolved, should be placed under suitable conditions, and it will then go on increasing. The minutest portion of living matter really now contains implicitly, as it were in a microcosm, the complexity of chemical and physical combinations and the conditions which were necessary for the first production of life in the macrocosm, ánd it supplies these as the conditions of further vital transformations. In fact, nature having accomplished a result, does not need on each future occasion to go through the preliminary steps by which the result was first arrived at. And in this relation it is very interesting to observe how much use is made of the force supplied by the destruction of certain organic matter in raising other matter to a higher stage. It is supposed, for example, that urea is partly produced by the oxidation of an excess of so-called albuminous matters in the blood, without these having entered into the formation of tissue ; and the force thus supplied in the retrograde metamorphosis will be available, and probably is used, for the exaltation of other elements.

It needs but little consideration to see that the living cell cannot supply all the force which is used in increasing and advancing life—in the multiplication and transformation of cells ; heat and other external conditions are necessary, as being, so to speak, material for transformation. It is a mistake, however, to say, as some have said, that heat and external conditions determine the rate of growth. The rate of germination, for example, certainly varies according to external conditions, but the limits of variation are fixed by the inherent properties of the structure. The seeds of a begonia taken from the same pod will, as Mr. Paget has pointed out, germinate, some in a day, some at the end of a year, and some at various intermediate times, even when they are all placed under the same external conditions. And the same author has pointed out other indications of self-dependent time-rates in the lower organisms. There are, in fact, internal as well as external conditions of growth, and the former are the more important, for they are really the determining conditions. It is with the organic cell and its conditions as it is with the individual and his circumstances; the latter may greatly modify character, and are necessary for development, but the essential fact, which determines the limit of the modifying power of circumstances, is the nature implanted in the individual.

It is easy to perceive how impossible it is, in the present state of science, to come to any positive conclusion with regard to the nature of the vital force. All that can be said is, that advancing knowledge more and more clearly proves the dependence of life on physical and chemical processes, and tends to show that vital action does not contrast with the kind of action exhibited by inorganic nature. Living matter displays, in fact, the

energy of colloidal and the plan of crystalloidal matter.
When vital force undergoes resolution into inferior force,
simultaneously with the decomposition of substance, it is
into heat, chemical force, and electricity that we find it,
as it were, unfolded; it is a natural conjecture, therefore,
that the conditions of the artificial production of vitality
must be a high and complex chemistry to represent the
statical correlative, and some mode of repulsion force, as
heat or electricity, or both, to represent the dynamical
correlative. It is certainly extremely unphilosophical in
the present condition of knowledge to refuse to accept
vitality as a special mode of manifestation of force; the
special character of its phenomena demand that, whatever its real nature may be, vital force should for the
present be received as a distinct force on the same terms
as chemical force or electrical force. The facts of
observation, as well as *a priori* considerations, unquestionably demand also that it should be regarded as
subject to the laws of the correlation and conservation
of force.

As then vital force is plainly by far the highest force
in dignity, a small quantity of it will correspond in value
to a much greater quantity of an inferior force; one
equivalent of vital force, in fact, will correspond to many
equivalents of the lower forces. An immense amount of
force is required to raise matter from its elementary state
to that condition in which it is described as organic;
and the upward transformation evidently only takes place
through the intermediate action of chemical force. But
vital force surpasses chemical force apparently in as great

degree as chemical force surpasses physical force. How
great, then, must be its mechanical equivalent! Who can
measure the power of a great idea? Armies fight in
vain against it, and nations yield to its sway. What
wonder that life was the last and highest development of
nature, and that it was produced only after the inferior
forces had been long in existence! What ground,
furthermore, it might be asked, have we for supposing
that it is destined to be the last development of force?
Is it not possible that a still higher manifestation of force
than that which we call vital may ultimately result from
the complexity of forces and conditions which are now
present on earth? The hypothesis of Laplace was,
that in primæval times a large quantity of nebulous
matter was spread through space. This nebulous matter
was through gravitation aggregated into solid masses.
Immense heat must have been thus produced, and this
heat might then produce light, and develop electricity
as it does now when acting on the thermo-electric plates.
Electricity might appear again as heat or as light, or as
chemical force, as it does in the decomposing cell of a
voltaic battery. The correlation of these forces we are
able to trace now, and it is not difficult to conceive how
they mutually excited and affected one another in the
primæval times when the earth was, as we are told,
without form and void. But there was a time when no
life existed on the earth. So that as we can now obtain
one force from another up to the point where life begins,
when we are at fault, similarly considerable time elapsed
in nature before vital force followed on the physical and

chemical forces. Science may, then, claim that in its difficulty and delay it only reflects a corresponding difficulty in nature.

But there are other important considerations with regard to vitality. It does not follow because we recognize a special vital manifestation that there is but one kind thereof; it is in reality necessary to admit different degrees, if not different kinds, of vitality. As with organic matter so with organic force, we trace an advance from the most simple and general to the most complex and special. The tissue of the simple protozoon is uniform and exhibits no trace of structure; its active relations are equally simple. In the ascending scale of life continuous differentiation of tissue corresponds with increasing speciality and complexity of relation with the external, until in man we observe the highest example of a unity of organism proceeding from manifold varieties of elements, and of unity of action from the co-ordination of many forces. And as it is with the animal kingdom, so it is with the elementary structures which form it; there is a scale of dignity, a hierarchy of tissues; the lowest appear first, and are necessary steps for the evolution of the highest. All the force of nature could not develop a nerve-cell directly out of inorganic matter; and the cell of the *Protococcus nivalis*, or the molecules of the Amœba, could not, under any possible circumstances, energize as nerve force. Between the vitality of thought and the vitality of the fungus there is scarcely a comparison possible; the former is dependent upon the widest and most complex, and at the same time the most intense and

special relations with external nature, while the latter
exhibits only a few general and comparatively simple relations therewith. Between the relations of a nerve-cell
and an epidermic cell with their surroundings, there is
as much difference as there is between the relations of
a Rhizopod and those of a Cephalopod with external
nature. And the relations of a nerve-cell with its surroundings are, it must be remembered, dependent on the
maintenance of the relations of all the inferior elements
of the body which intervene in the descending scale
between it and the inorganic.

Whatever, then, may be the fact in animal development, it is certain that transformation of species takes
place in the structural elements. When a tissue takes
material from the blood, it does not merely aggregate,
but it assimilates it—that is, it makes it of the same *kind*
with itself. In development, a higher tissue constantly
proceeds from a lower one, and demands the lower one
as a necessary antecedent to its production ; it has thus,
as external conditions, not only those which are general,
but the intimate and special influences of the tissue which
is before it in the order of existence. In the latter are
supplied the special and essential conditions for the
exaltation and transpeciation of force and material. But
all exaltation of force is, as it were, a concentration of it ;
one equivalent of the higher force corresponds to many
equivalents of the inferior force which has been transformed. Hence it is that the power of reproducing
tissues or parts in animals is diminished much more
by development than by growth ; and the law which

describes the reparative power in each species of animal
as being in an inverse ratio to its position in the scale of
life, though not strictly proved, is yet true as a general
proposition.

If, now, the degree of dignity of an element represents
a corresponding degree of vitality, it is obviously right
to speak of the life of the blood, without any design of
placing its life on the same level with that of nerve.   In
the decomposition of material and the correlative resolution of force which take place when the blood-cell
returns to the inorganic state, there will be much less
force liberated than when a nerve-cell undergoes the
retrograde metamorphosis.   As a great expenditure of
force is needed to raise matter from the inorganic to the
organic state, so a further greater expenditure is required
to raise matter from a low organic to its highest organic
condition.   The nerve-cell is, so to say, the highest
parasite which thus sucks up the life of the blood ; and
if the process of its decomposition were accurately
observed, it would be found that all the force which had
been consumed by it in its upward transformation was
given back to nature in its downward metamorphosis.

The retrograde metamorphosis of organic elements is
constantly taking place as a part of the history of life.
In the function of nerve-cell, a nerve-force is liberated
which excites muscular force, and is ultimately given back
to external nature as motion ; the coincident "waste" of
substance is received into the blood and ultimately also
passes back to nature.   It is probable, however, that this
"waste" does not pass always directly out of the body,

but that it may be first used as the nutriment of some lower element. Thus, as there seemed reason to believe that, in the economy of nature, animal matter did not undergo the extreme retrograde metamorphosis into inorganic matter before being used as food by vegetables, so in the animal body the higher elements do not appear at once to undergo the extreme retrograde metamorphosis, but are first used as the nutriment of lower organic element. How admirably does nature thus economize in the body! Just as on a larger scale the carbonic acid exhaled by animals is taken up by vegetables, and a poison thus removed from the atmosphere in which the animal lives, so by one organic element of the body the blood is purified from the waste matter of a higher element which would be poisonous to it.

The parts impaired by activity, as all parts must be, are repaired during rest in a condition of health. And it is very interesting to observe, as Mr. Paget has pointed out, that the organic processes of repair in each tissue are adjusted to a certain time-rate, which is variable according to, but is not determined by, external conditions. The time-rate is determined by the implanted properties, and "for each unit of nutrition might be reckoned a unit of time." The periodicities of organic life appear to be prominent instances of the law; and the rhythmic motions of the heart, or the motions of cilia, are, Mr. Paget supposes, due "to a method of nutrition in which the acting parts are, at certain periods, raised with time-regulated progress to a state of instability of composition from which they then decline, and in their decline may

N

change their shape and move with a definite velocity, or (as nervous centres) may discharge nerve-force."[1] In this recognition of the chronometry of organic processes, there is unquestionably great promise for the future; for it is plain that the observance of time in the motions of organic molecules is as certain and universal, if not as exact, as that in the motions of heavenly bodies. Each organic process has its definite time-rate; and each cell has its appointed period of life different for different kinds of cells. The exercise of its energy is the accomplishment of the life-task of the gland-cell of the stomach, and its existence ends therewith—it discharges its duty with its life; but it is not so with other cells. It is not known, for example, how soon the blood-cell and other cells die. The blood-cell may be ephemeral, and after the manufacture of its material straightway perish, supplying in the products of its decomposition material for the colouring matters of the bile; or it may accomplish its function more than once, and live therefore for some time. Certain facts do, indeed, point to a short duration, as, for example, the destruction of the nucleus in the blood-cell, the analogy of the cells of the stomach and milk glands, and of the sebaceous and spermatic cells, and the great production of blood-cells; but nothing positive is known, and the subject is one which awaits, and ought to receive, careful attention.

Such, then, is the general process of life physiologically regarded. But there is nothing special in disease.

[1] On the Chronometry of Life. By J. Paget, F.R.S. (Croonian Lecture before the Royal Society, 1857.)

Although the destructive cancerous mass seems at first sight to admit of no sort of comparison with the beneficial formation of a developing organ, yet the production is governed by laws of organic growth and activity. No new forces nor new laws appear in the organism under the circumstances which are described as disease. "'Tis as natural to die as to be born," says Sir T. Browne; and if we choose to accept the doctrine of final cause, we must acknowledge that the disease which leads to death is as natural, as much in the purpose of nature, as the physiological processes which constitute health. An individual exists in certain relations with the external, and the harmony which results from the maintenance of these relations is health, while a disturbance of them, whether from a cause in the organism or in the external circumstances, or partly in one and partly in the other, is discord or disease. The phenomena of morbid action may therefore, when properly regarded, be serviceable as experiments illustrating the character and relations of vital action.

As each cell has its appointed period of life, and each species of cell its natural degree of life, and as there are many cells and many kinds of cells in the human body, it is evident that disease will be more easily initiated in it than in an organism with less differentiation of tissue, and less complexity of structure. For the life of the organism is the sum of the life of its individual parts, and superiority of vitality signifies more numerous, special, and complex relations with the external. In the lowest organisms, where there is a similarity of structure, one part is independent of another, and dependent only on the maintenance of certain general and simple relations with the external; there is, therefore, comparatively little liability to disturbance.[1] When the parts are, however, unlike, and there is a definite subordination of them, so that the well-being of the highest structure is dependent on the well-being of all the structures which intervene in the descending scale between it and inorganic nature, there is plainly abundant room for disturbance. As in the state, so in the organism, the vitality of the government flows from, and rests upon, the well-being of individuals.

When, from some of the many disturbing causes which initiate disease, a particular elementary constituent of the body is prevented from rising to the dignity of its specific constitution and energy, there will, if the disturbing cause has not been so serious as to destroy the life of the part, be a production of an element of a lower kind with a lower energy; and that is a diseased product. It is as if the substance of a polype were produced amongst the higher physiological elements of the human body, and went on increasing there without regard to relations with surrounding elements of tissue. There may be a pro-

---

[1] Goethe, after saying that everything living is a collection of living self-dependent beings, adds, "Je unvolkommner das Geschöpf ist, desto mehr sind diese Theile einander gleich oder ähnlich, und desto mehr gleichen sie dem Ganzen. Je volkommner das Geschöpf wird, desto unähnlicher werden die Theile einander. Je ähnlicher die Theile einander sind, desto weniger sind sie einander subordinirt. Die Subordination der Theile deutet auf ein volkommneres Geschöpf."

duction of foreign substance in larger quantity than that which should rightly be formed of the natural tissue, and a greater display of force, but both structure and energy are of a lower order. What is gained in quantity is lost in quality, and the vitality is intrinsically less.

Inflammation in a part is really the result of a degeneration of its vitality. When a wound heals by the " first intention," there is direct adhesion of its surfaces, and no inflammation, for the natural vitality of the part is maintained, and effects the repair. When slight inflammation occurs, the vitality of the part has undergone a certain degeneration, and material of an inferior order to the proper element of the part is produced; this substance binds the surfaces together, and it may in process of time, on the complete subsidence of inflammation, and under the favourable conditions of surrounding healthy tissue life, even rise to the condition of the proper structure. But the lymph does not appear to be thrown out with any special beneficial design; it is the simple result of a deterioration of energy, is only a less degree of a positive evil. When greater inflammation takes place, or when the natural vitality of the part is feeble, there is a greater degeneration, and material of a still lower kind, which is not even organizable under any circumstances, is produced. Pus is poured out, and ceases to appear with the restoration of the proper vitality of the tissue. If the inflammation is still greater, the degeneration passes into actual destruction of life, and mortification ensues. When John Hunter, therefore, speaks, as he does, of nature calling up the vital powers to produce suppuration, his words convey a false notion of what really happens. The injury has so damaged the parts that the vital action cannot rise to its specific elevation; an inferior kind of action is alone possible, which is really disease, and only so far beneficial as it proves that the life of the part has not been killed outright. As might be expected, therefore, it is in exhausting diseases that inflammation most commonly and easily occurs. How incorrect, then, is it to speak of inflammation as if it were a process specially provided for restoring the healthy life of parts ! When adhesive inflammation is said to limit the suppuration of an abscess, its occurrence is a result of diminishing mischief, and testifies to a less serious degeneration of vital force. How hard it is not to be blind when theories or wishes lead us ! When adhesive inflammation fixes à piece of strangulated gut to the side of the belly, so as happily to prevent the passage of fæcal matter into the peritoneal cavity, it is sometimes said to be a wise and kindly provision of nature. What, then, shall be said of inflammation when it glues the gut to a hernial cavity, or manufactures a fibrous band which strangles the gut? Is this also wise and beneficial design ?

That which is true of the material products of inflammation is necessarily true of its force; the heat and pain, and rigors, the forces as well as the material, testify to a degeneration of vital force. The sort of stormy rage and demonstrative activity which characterize inflammation, though unquestionably an exhibition of force, are not really an increased display of the proper vital force. The latter has undergone a transformation from the quiet self-contained activity of development into the unrestrained dissipation of a lower activity; and, as regards the latter, it might be said that several monads of its matter, or volumes of its force, are equivalent only to one monad of matter or one volume of force of the former. Rigors, as the involuntary action of voluntary muscle, are a degradation of action witnessing to a molecular deterioration of vital conditions. Heat is a physical force which must have resulted from the retrograde metamorphosis of vital force. The existence of pain where rightly there should be no sensation, testifies to a molecular deterioration of statical element and a correlative exhibition of force. The increased action of inflammation in a part is, therefore, diminished vital action. Perhaps it might once for all be stated, as a law of vital action, that the dignity of the force is in an inverse ratio to its volumetrical display. It is indeed with organic action as it is with mental action. The emotional man displays considerable force, and often produces great effects in the way of destruction, but his power is vastly inferior to that of the man who has developed emotional force into the higher form of will-force, who has co-ordinated the passions into the calm, self-contained activity of definite productive aim. Surely creation always testifies to a much higher energy than destruction.

The foregoing considerations unavoidably flow from a conception of vitality as correlate with other natural forces, and as subject to the law of the conservation of force. They obtain additional weight, however, from being in some accordance with the important generalizations which one of the most philosophical physiologists of the present time has made with regard to morbid products. Virchow has, as is well known, referred all morbid structures to physiological types, and maintains that there is no new structure produced in the organism by disease. The cancer-cell, the pus-cell, and all other disease-produced cells, have their patterns in the cells of healthy structure. The cells of tubercle correspond with the corpuscles of the lymphatic glands ; pus and colourless blood-corpuscles cannot be distinguished except by looking at the place whence they come ; the cells of cancer in bone "are the immediate descendants of the cells in bone ;" and certain colloid tumours have the structure of the umbilical cord. "Where a new formation takes place, certain histological elements of the body must generally also cease to exist ;" and every kind of new formation is really, therefore, destructive, and destroys something of what previously existed. The connective tissue, with its equivalents, he describes as the common stock of germs of the body ; from them morbid structures proceed by continuous development. "Heterologous tissues have physiological types ; and there is no other kind of heterology in morbid structures than the abnormal manner in which they arise as to place (heterotopia), time (heterochronia), and quantity (heterometria)."[1]

[1] Cellular Pathology.

The conclusions with regard to vital force, which a consistent conception of it as a natural force seems to necessitate, will find extensive application in the various phenomena of disease. We have seen that if the resolution of the vitality of a single nerve-cell into a vitality of a lower kind be supposed,—into that, for example, of polype substance,—it would necessarily suffice for the production of a whole polype, or perhaps of a multitude of polypes. In other words, one nervous unit, monad, or molecule, is the vital equivalent of many units, monads, or molecules of polype substance. How idle it is, then, to dispute, as some have done, as to whether epilepsy is increased vital action or diminished vital action, when there exists no clear conception of what is meant by the words ! No one can deny that there is great display of force in the convulsions of epilepsy, but is it increased vital force ? Is a man in convulsions a strong man? for that is the real question. Does convulsion in a paralysed limb indicate increased vital action of it ? When tetanus of a muscle is produced, as Weber showed it might be, by putting a loop of thread round its nerve and slowly and gradually tightening it, does the violent action of the muscle testify to increased vitality? If it really does, then the mechanical tetanomotor of Heidenhain might, properly used, suffice for the cure of every paralysis, and effect a complete renewal of life.

In speaking of vital action, we may either consider the whole organism as individual, or we may consider the cell or organic monad as the individual. If we regard the organism as individual, then when general convulsions take place in it—that is, violent and aimless movements completely withdrawn from the control of the will, which should rightly co-ordinate them into definite action—it is simply to use words without meaning to say that the vital action of the individual is increased. There is not, then, individual action; and the definition of vitality is not applicable to the organism as a whole. The highest manifestation of individuality is in the consciousness of man, the so-called unity of the ego; but when the co-ordination of forces for a definite end is replaced by the convulsions of epilepsy, there is neither subjective nor objective unity of action. Instead of that quiet will-force which expresses conscious unity, or that unconscious unity of organic action which is manifest in sleep, there is the violent and incoherent exhibition of inferior force. Increased action is the result of a degeneration of the proper vital action. " A man in convulsions is not strong, though six men cannot hold him."

Like considerations apply when the single cell is regarded as individual. In virtue of a certain chemical constitution and a certain definite arrangement of molecules, a cell exhibits energy as nerve force. That special mode of energy is the definite result of a certain co-ordination of chemical combinations and molecular relations; and these are connoted in the individuality of the cell. When, however, in place of the definite process of statical attraction (nutrition) and dynamical

repulsion (energy), there takes place a large demonstrative display of force,—as general epileptic convulsions, being the sum of the action of the individual
cells, prove there must,—it is impossible to pronounce
such force as of the same rank or kind as the proper
energy of the cell. It is an inferior kind of power, and
the certain indication of a degeneration of the statical
correlative. It is the duty of a cell, so to speak,
as of an individual, to live in certain relations with its
surroundings—it is, indeed, its essence as an *individual*
cell of specific character ; and when it is not so living,
it is really degenerating, losing its nature or kind,
passing more or less quickly towards death. Its action
is certainly not increased functional action. In truth,
it would be as just to call the extravagant action of
madness in an individual occupying a certain position
in a system of government increased functional action,
and to say that the government was stronger for his
degenerate action. A state, again, would not be powerful, would not even exist, if each individual did as his
passions prompted, altogether regardless of his relations
to others ; and it would certainly be a strange use of
language to say then that the functional action of that
individual was increased.

The phenomena of conscious vitality might be used
to illustrate the same principles. A passionate man
is not strong-minded, nor do the ravings of insanity
reveal mental vigour. A completely-fashioned will is
the true mark of a strong mind. " A character," said
Novalis, " is a completely-fashioned will." As in the

order of natural development there has been an ascent from the physical and chemical forces to the aim-working vital force, and thence from the lowest vitality to the highest manifestation thereof, so in the course of mental development there is a progress through sensation, passion, emotion, reason, to the highest phase of mental force, a well-fashioned will. The rightly-developed mind, like the healthy cell, recognizes its relations to others; self-feeling gives place to or expands into moral feeling, and in the will all the phases of consciousness are co-ordinated into calm, just, definite action. Noise and fury surely indicate weakness; they are the manifestation of inferior force—the tale of an idiot signifying nothing. The strongest force is quiet force, and the ravings of insanity, which might not unjustly be compared to the convulsions of epilepsy, do not evince mental power.

May we not, then, already perceive, what advancing knowledge must ever render more clear, how the conscious mind of man blends in unity of development with the unconscious life of nature? As the revelation of nature proceeds in the progress of science, the idealism of Plato and the realism of Bacon will be found to harmonize as expressions of the same truths; the generalizations of Humboldt and the poetical intuitions of Goethe may be looked upon as but different descriptions of the same facts. Idealism and realism blend and are extinguished in the intimate harmony between the individual and nature. How great, then, the ignorance which fancies that poetry demands a rude age for its successful development! How little, again, the insight which would make of science an ugly anatomy only! After analysis comes synthesis; and beyond the practical realization of science in works which add to human comfort, there remains the æsthetical embodiment of science. Art has now opening before it a field so wide that imagination cannot dare to limit it, for science must plainly attain to its highest development in the work of the future poet, who shall give to its reality a beautiful form. Goethe indicated the path, but he who shall accomplish it will be a greater than Goethe.[1]

---

[1] Perhaps the truest estimate of science, and the most remarkable prophecy with regard to it, is to be found in that wonderful tale by Goethe, "Das Mährchen," a tale which has been described by one who has done most towards making Goethe known and understood in England, " as the deepest poem of its sort in existence—as the only true prophecy emitted for who knows how many centuries."

THE END.

LONDON:
R. CLAY, SONS, AND TAYLOR, PRINTERS,
BREAD STREET HILL.

For EU product safety concerns, contact us at Calle de José Abascal, 56–1°,
28003 Madrid, Spain or eugpsr@cambridge.org.

 www.ingramcontent.com/pod-product-compliance
Ingram Content Group UK Ltd.
Pitfield, Milton Keynes, MK11 3LW, UK
UKHW012346130625
459647UK00009B/572